INGMAR BERGMAN:
THE CINEMA AS MISTRESS

🞐🞐🞐🞐🞐🞐🞐🞐🞐🞐

INGMAR BERGMAN:

THE CINEMA AS MISTRESS

Philip Mosley

🞐🞐🞐🞐🞐🞐🞐🞐🞐🞐

MARION BOYARS

LONDON · BOSTON

Published in Great Britain and the United States in 1981
by Marion Boyars Publishers Ltd
18 Brewer Street, London W1R 4AS
and Marion Boyars Publishers Inc.
99 Main Street, Salem, New Hampshire 03079

Australian and New Zealand distribution by Thomas C. Lothian
4-12 Tattersalls Lane, Melbourne, Victoria 3000

British Library Cataloguing in Publication Data

Moseley, Philip
   Ingmar Bergman.
   I. Title
   791.43'0233   PN1998.A3.B/

ISBN 0-7145-2644-4

Library of Congress Catalog Card Number 79-56841

Typeset by John Smith, London
Printed in Great Britain by The Anchor Press Ltd
and bound by Wm Brendon & Son Ltd
both of Tiptree, Essex

Contents

Chapter 3

Chapter 4

For Melvin J. Friedman

The theatre is like a loyal wife, film is the
big adventure, the expensive and demanding
mistress – you worship both, each in its
own way.
(Bergman, 1950)

Filmscripts by Ingmar Bergman
published by Marion Boyars Publishers:

A FILM TRILOGY:

    Through a Glass Darkly
    The Communicants (Winter Light)
    The Silence

PERSONA and SHAME

FOUR STORIES:

    The Touch
    Cries and Whispers
    Hour of the Wolf
    The Passion (The Passion of Anna)

FACE TO FACE

SCENES FROM A MARRIAGE

THE SERPENT'S EGG

Preface
and Acknowledgements

Where published texts in English are not available, quotations from films are taken from viewings. This includes those films published as *Four Stories* by Ingmar Bergman (London, Marion Boyars Publishers 1977), except for quotations from *A Passion* which are my translations of the French text published in *L'Avant-Scène du Cinéma*, 109 (December, 1970). British film titles are used. American titles (where different) are listed in the filmography.

My greatest debt is to John Fletcher who gave a guiding hand in establishing the shape of the book and drafted the Introduction and the short essays on *The Seventh Seal, Hour of the Wolf, The Silence, Shame* and Bergman in television. My special thanks to Daniel MacLennan, whose knowledge of Bergman's early work was generously placed at my disposal and forms the basis of the chapter, *The Early Films*. Members of John Fletcher's seminar on 'Strindberg and Bergman', at the University of East Anglia in 1972, especially Alan Pulverness, contributed ideas incorporated at various places in the text.

For quotations from copyright material, grateful acknowledgement is made to Marion Boyars Ltd and to Lorrimer Publishing Ltd. Photographs are reproduced by permission.

Parts of John Fletcher's contribution to the book first appeared in *Journal of Modern Literature*, III, 2 (April 1973), 173-90, and *UEA Film*, n.d., 1-3.

The book aims at the ground between academic studies and film journalism, and offers a fairly complete survey; I have in mind particularly the experienced but eclectic cinema-goer who, having seen most of Bergman's major films, would appreciate an informed view of their context and significance.

Finally, my warm thanks to Catherine Shinners and Carol Scales for help with the typing.

PM

Biographical Note

Ingmar Bergman was born in Uppsala, Sweden, on 14 July 1918. His father was a Lutheran pastor. He studied at Stockholm University and in 1938 made his debut as an amateur director at Master Olofsgården Theatre in Stockholm. In 1944 he became a professional director, working for two years at the City Theatres in Hälsingborg and Malmö. From 1946 he spent most of his time working at Gothenburg City Theatre until he moved back to Malmö City Theatre in 1952. In 1959 he became director at the Royal Dramatic Theatre in Stockholm, where he served as head from 1963-66.

In 1944 he wrote his first filmscript for *Frenzy (Hets)*, directed by Alf Sjöberg. Bergman's first feature film was *Crisis (Kris)*, released in 1945 and based on the play *The Mother Creature (Moderdyret)* by the Danish author Leck Fischer. *Prison (Fängelse,* 1949) was the first film written and directed by Bergman. Since *Crisis* he has directed almost forty films and had a hand in the making of several others.

Until trouble with the Swedish authorities uprooted him, Bergman lived on the island of Fårö, adjacent to Gotland in the Baltic Sea. A number of his more recent films were made there. He lived and worked in West Germany for several years and then returned to Sweden.

Outline Filmography

Date	English Titles*	Swedish Titles and Other Details
1944	Frenzy (Torment)	Hets (*Script and Assistant Director to Sjöberg*)
1945	Crisis	Kris
1946	It Rains on Our Love	Det regnar på vår kärlek
1947	Woman Without a Face	Kvinna utan ansikte (*Script*)
1947	A Ship to India (The Land of Desire)	Skepp till Indialand
1947	Night is My Future (Music in Darkness)	Musik i mörker
1948	Port of Call	Hamnstad
1948	Eva	Eva (*Script, with Molander*)
1949	Prison (The Devil's Wanton)	Fängelse
1949	Thirst (Three Strange Loves)	Törst
1949	To Joy	Till glädje
1950	While the City Sleeps	Medan staden sover (*Script synopsis*)
1950	This Can't Happen Here (High Tension)	Sånt händer inte här
1950	Summer Interlude (Illicit Interlude)	Sommarlek
1951	Divorced	Frånskild (*Script, with Grevenius*)
1952	Waiting Woman (Secrets of Women)	Kvinnors väntan
1952	Summer with Monika (Monika)	Sommaren med Monika

* British first, with American in parentheses if different.

CHAPTER ONE

THE NORDIC ANGLE

Exhibitioner and Exhibitionist

> *Through over-exposure words like*
> *emptiness, loneliness, strangeness,*
> *pain and helplessness have lost their*
> *force.* (Persona)

In the short essay on film-making published with the script of *Wild
Strawberries* (*Smultronstället*), Ingmar Bergman makes two statements which may seem contradictory. He first of all asserts: 'Film
has nothing to do with literature; the character and substance of
the two art forms are usually in conflict.' On the next page he
writes: 'In my own life, my great literary influence was Strindberg.
There are works of his which can still make my hair stand on end.'
The debt to Strindberg, openly acknowledged here and elsewhere,
is so evident throughout his work that those critics, mainly Swedish, who have condemned his films as 'borrowed and edited Strindberg', have cracked a nut with a sledgehammer and missed the real
point. Had Bergman a less acute sense of the essential distinction
between literature, even drama, and the cinema, he might well, as
a Swede steeped in Swedish culture, have made films that were
little more than screen adaptations of Strindberg's plays.

   We must not underestimate the debt which his early works owe
to such diverse sources as the silent Swedish film classics of Stiller
and Sjöstrom, to the French films of the Carné-Duvivier vintage,
and to Italian neo-realism; nor can we overlook what he has learned
about tempo, rhythm, and long-shot from middle-period Antonioni and which he has applied in his more recent productions. As a
film-maker Bergman is largely self-taught. He had a thorough
grounding in dramatic art through his long experience as resident
director at the city theatres of Hälsingborg, Gothenburg, and

Malmö, but in the world of motion pictures he picked things up as
he went along. In his younger days he was an inveterate and
apparently indiscriminate film-goer. He warmly acknowledges the
apprentice training he received as a novice director at the hands of
Alf Sjöberg, who directed his first script *Frenzy* in 1944, and from
Lorens Marmstedt, the producer of four of his early films, including *Prison*.

It is quite clear that with this somewhat haphazard education in
cinematics Bergman is neither a professional of the American
variety, nor is he the sort of theorist and critic turned film-maker
characterized by the *Cahiers du cinéma* circle in France, particularly
Godard, Doniol-Valcroze and Rohmer. He is basically an artist of
live drama with extensive practical experience in stage production.
He is not a playwright – the plays he has written are mediocre – but
he *is* a theatrical director of genius. His stage interpretations of
Goethe, Ibsen and Strindberg have been seen and acclaimed inter-
nationally, and particularly in Malmö he brought together a group
of actors (such as Ingrid Thulin and Max von Sydow) whose
ensemble playing attained such technical perfection that Bergman
has been able, in his greatest films, to employ them in different
combinations over and over again. Several members of this 'stable',
in fact, are numbered among the very finest actors working anywhere today. But the truly remarkable thing is that, unlike most
theatre people, he is transformed into an authentic cineast the
moment he steps on to the set. The reason for this lies firstly in his
sensitivity to rhythmic effects of light and sound: in the essay
'Bergman Discusses Film-Making' Bergman gives a striking
account of how on sunny afternoons in Uppsala, Venice seemed to
come alive in his grandmother's flat. It lies secondly in his awareness of the expressive potential of the human face, which the
close-up camera expands to fill the whole space of the sharply-lit
screen, holding the spectator's full attention. He has, of course,
been well-served by expert directors of photography, the brilliant
Gunnar Fischer and Sven Nykvist.

Bergman's composition and lighting differ radically in style
according to choice of cameraman. Many of the earlier films were
photographed by Gunnar Fischer who favoured strong lighting

and effects of high contrast. 'His lighting and close-ups in, for example, *The Face*, are inextricably bound up with his conception of Bergman and of Bergman's movies', writes Marianne Höök, and there is evidence that his role was much more dominant than that of Sven Nykvist, director of photography in the later movies from *The Virgin Spring (Jungfrukällan)* onwards. In *Bergman on Bergman* the director blames his own increasingly tyrannical attitude for the ending of the collaboration between Gunnar Fischer and himself; but it is clear that Fischer had his own ideas and views of what a film should look like and these became more and more constricting to Bergman. On the other hand, the relationship with Nykvist is, according to the director, largely intuitive: 'the impulse comes from me', he says, 'and the enormously careful, subtle, and technically clever execution is all Sven Nykvist's work' (p. 35). Certainly, Nykvist's style — even allowing for the availability of faster and more sensitive film stock — is very different from Fischer's. In marked contrast to his predecessor's sharply differentiated blacks and whites, Nykvist has evolved a largely shadowless light which he refers to as 'granite tone' (*American Cinematographer*, October 1962, p. 628), photography without extreme contrasts, simple and naturalistic in effect.

For a long time Bergman resisted colour film; he did not need it. His black and white had a 'pronounced sense of colour effect' (Marianne Höök). His first essay in polychrome was *Now About These Woman (För att inte tala om alla dessa kvinnor)* which shows an interesting use of pastel effects; *Cries and Whispers (Viskningar och rop)* makes eloquent play with different shades of red; and the sheep sequences in *Faro Document (Fårö-dokument)* are done in colour to highlight the grisly naturalism of the lambing and slaughtering scenes, whereas the interviews with the islanders are filmed in monochrome of a rather sepia quality. And the grainy colour of the closing minutes of *A Passion (En Passion)* contributes not a little to the overwhelmingly moving quality of the sequence. As James F. Scott so pertinently remarks, 'for this director, technique is always dramatically functional'. Bergman lays down the general style his technicians follow; and above all, he has for many years now written his own scripts. He began to do so, he tells us, because of the lack of suitable material, and indeed the films he has made from commissioned scenarios, such as Ulla Isaksson's *So Close to Life* (*Nära livet*) and *The Virgin Spring*, are not to be numbered among his masterpieces.

Though this might appear to conflict with the fact that Bergman is by his own admission not a good writer, this is not the case. His published scripts consist largely of discursive prose aimed at 'fixing' the initial impression and giving some guide to the way the movie should eventually be filmed. The fact that this material has an 'indicative' function rather than a prescriptive one is shown by the frequency of non-visual asides, such as remarks about perfumes or smells, or comments suggesting a psychological interpretation which by definition cannot be transferred to the screen. The dialogue itself is often marked by flatness and banality, and one can understand why it is possible for native Swedes to make fun of it, particularly when it is quoted out of context. If we nonetheless experience vivid emotion on reading the scripts of *The Seventh Seal, The Silence* (*Tystnaden*) or *Persona* (*Persona*), this is because they recall for us, however imperfectly, the memory of the original cinema experience, and not because of any intrinsic merit they possess. This is less true of Bergman's more strictly fictional works, the *Four Stories*, which are not so much screenplays as narratives which served as the basis for the films concerned (*The Touch* (*Beröringen*) *Cries and Whispers, Hour of the Wolf* (*Vargtimmen*) and *A Passion*). They exist in another dimension and extend the meaning of the film; in the case of *The Touch*, the psychology of the lovers, especially their hatred and self-hatred, is explored in a discursive and elucidatory manner which adds considerably to our understanding not only of the film as screened, but also of the reasons for its relative failure, the chief of which was the miscasting of Elliott Gould. What the prose conveys – far more poignantly than the film – is the bleak but overwhelming vision that to love is to suffer, and that the more intense the love the more excruciating is the suffering. People are cruel, Bergman shows us, and rarely more so than to those whom they love and who love them. A man like David can only wound the loved one while he feels strong, but cringes before her when he is weak; yet sometimes he affords her tender and exquisite moments which, however fleetingly, make it all seem worth while.

Bergman's scripts should not be judged by criteria appropriate to more explicitly literary works. A Bergman text is only a sketch for another and quite different creation: the finished film. Bergman took to writing his own texts not because he had literary aspirations (or if he did, he soon lost them), but because other people's scripts did not deal with the subjects, problems and themes in which he was interested. And he has been extremely fortunate – as he himself recognizes – in the backing he has received for these projects in the past from Swedish film producers, notably Carl Anders Dymling, thanks to whom, he writes, 'I am able to work with an integrity that has become the very air I breathe, and one of the main reasons I do not want to work outside Sweden'. He modestly adds, 'my only significance in the world of film lies in the freedom of my creativity'. Certainly he has been fortunate in having such a free hand to 'perform conjuring tricks with apparatus so expensive and so wonderful that any entertainer in history would have given anything to have it.' Bergman has thus been remarkably free of the pressures towards compromise which have warped so many talents in the history of the industry. He has taken maximum advantage of the privilege.

So we have, in Ingmar Bergman, a working artist of the theatre whose creative drive, together with a good deal of luck, has led to the making of a number of films which stand clearly within the Swedish literary tradition deriving from Strindberg. Several critics have noted this relationship but few have explored it at any depth.

August Strindberg, who died in 1912 (six years before Bergman was born), is one of the most influential figures in the literary and artistic movement which Frank Kermode has termed 'paleo-modernism'; that is the first modernist generation which arose before the turn of the century and declined soon after the First World War. Bergman, on the other hand, is, in Kermode's opinion, a leading representative of 'neo-modernism', the moder-nist revival in the period following World War II. Thus Strindberg died while the cinema was still in its infancy and its potentialities were not yet realized, although there is evidence that the ageing playwright took a distinct interest in it. Very much an all-rounder as an author, and a prolific one at that (his collected works in Swedish run to nearly sixty volumes), he was all his life primarily interested in dramatic art. Not only did he move in theatrical circles (two of his wives were actresses), he also wrote a number of essays (notably the early *Foreword to Miss Julie* and later the *Open Letters to the Intimate Theatre*) which constitute major contributions to the theory of dramatic art. Thus he had a well-developed sense of practicalities which helps explain why even his more fantastical plays have survived, whereas those of other contemporaries, like Maeterlinck, have not. Even in his wilder moments he was concerned with expanding the resources of the stage and developing its expressive capacity, forcing it to adopt new forms which have continued to dominate the experimental theatre ever since. Without Strindberg's example, Cocteau and Adamov, Albee, Pinter, and a host of others, could not have written the way they do. This is particularly true of Strindberg's dialogue and characterization: speech in his plays follows a logic of its own and is little influenced by the relevance criterion dear to the well-made play. His characters do not conform to the fixity of recognizable real-life models, but are invariably larger than life, as unpredictable and changing as their creator. It would appear that such innovations came quite naturally to Strindberg. He wrote intuitively, and was not fussy about tying up loose ends, often not bothering to take minor characters off stage once he had brought them on. His producers have to write in many of the necessary stage-directions, and even ignore those that make nonsense of the action. The whole of Strindberg's attention was concentrated on developing the situation in the play as swiftly, economically and plausibly as possible, and he had no energy to spare for textual minutiae. In *Miss Julie*, for example, matters come to a head, and explode, in one fairly short act. *The Father*, too, moves at a rapid pace. The length of a Strindberg play – its pure performance time – is usually in inverse proportion to the strength of the impact it makes on the audience. And the techniques which Strindberg adopted intuitively in this way have been very consciously taken over by later playwrights.

They have likewise followed Strindberg's example by blurring the distinction (previously considered sacrosanct) between dream and reality. Ionesco in particular has made almost a trade-mark of the manner in which his plays veer off into the fantastical soon after they begin: a case in point is *Victims of Duty*, where the cosy after-dinner chat of the Choubert couple rapidly degenerates into a parable of violence and subjection. This occurs more subtly in Pinter's *The Homecoming* where the wife of returning Englishman Teddy gradually becomes involved in and fascinated by his family until, mesmerized, she abandons her children, cuts herself loose from all her American ties, and agrees to work as a call-girl in the employ of her husband's father and brothers. The play thus becomes a complex study of male fantasies, but even at its most improbable never loses its credibility, so ably-contrived and redolent of contemporary London are the setting and the characterization.

Strindberg was also among the first dramatists to blur the distinction between past and present time. Here too he has been followed by contemporary playwrights. In Samuel Beckett's radio play, *Embers,* for instance, Henry is abruptly transported back twenty years by the associations set up in his mind by the wifely command 'Don't!'. Beckett's point is satirical and mildly smutty, but it derives very clearly from Strindberg's indifference to traditional chronology and his tendency to superimpose past on present time. It is inevitable that Bergman, too, should adopt all these features in his films. This snatch of dialogue from *Shame* could almost have been lifted from Strindberg and could, similarly, have occurred in one of Harold Pinter's plays:

> *Jan comes down the stairs, greets Jacobi cordially and asks how things are.*
> JACOBI: Bad. I've just had a letter from my wife. She's in Switzerland.
> EVA: Not bad news, I hope?
> JACOBI: Why should there be bad news? Good God, no. Everything's going splendidly. We'll have real

> peace within the half-year. There's a cease-fire all the
> way, and both parties — well, you've got the radio.
> You know.
> EVA: I meant your wife. No bad news from your wife.
> JACOBI: I brought something to drink with me. A
> bottle of Renault Carte Noir. What do you say?
> Have you got some glasses? Eva darling, you're more
> beautiful every day. Can't you leave this half-wit
> you're married to and come to me instead? I'm much
> better, I promise you. In every way. (*Persona and
> Shame*, p. 161)

Aside from the fact that Jacobi is drunk, there is logic of a kind in
his apparent non sequiturs: he is infatuated with Eva, and is afraid
of the partisans who are hiding in the woods and whose victim he is
soon to be. The words spoken reveal also his contempt for Jan both
as a man and a husband, although it is expressed jokingly and is
only heard behind the smoke-screen of polite enquiries after
Jacobi's wife. They also betray his deep fears about the civil war
situation: the 'bad'/'splendidly' contradiction gives this away. The
latent antagonisms, the hatreds and self-hatreds felt by this trio,
are palpable even in the script; the movie itself develops them with
great effect, incidentally underlining the irony of Jacobi's gift to
Jan of the Score of Dvorak's Trio in E flat major 'which one day we
can play together, all three of us'. All this testifies not only to the
way Bergman, like other contemporary artists, has learned Strindberg's lessons, but also to the fact, as he himself put it, that 'as a
film-maker I am conscientious, hard-working, and extremely careful; my films involve good craftsmanship, and my pride is the
pride of a good craftsman'.

Strindberg's influence is evident not only on the technical level in
Bergman's films. Both artists are figures of universal stature and
importance; they are among the few to have achieved fame and
recognition outside the confines of their own sprawling, thinly-
populated northern country of lake, island, pine and silver-birch.

Yet they are at the same time fundamentally and typically Swedish, best understood in the context of that culture, dominated as it
is by a harsh climate of long, dark winters and short, intense
summers, and marked too by the severity of Lutheran worship
overlaying a medieval Catholicism which itself only partially con-
cealed paganism conquered relatively late in the Church's history.
The bleakness of the climate and the sternness of the faith account
for much in the Swedish temperament: its desperation in the
taking of pleasures, together with a well-developed self-control
and corporate discipline; its dourness, its volatility, even its ever-
present guilty conscience based principally on a guilt-dominated
religion and exacerbated by the fact that a high standard of living
has been made possible by fairly ruthless capitalism and a free
market economy functioning at the expense of the third world. It
is, moreover, a pacifist country with a flourishing arms export
industry. Swedish moral self-righteousness understandably grates
on the ears of those to whom it is often so unhesitatingly directed,
and can appear, to sensitive Swedes, to have been too cheaply
acquired. So much that appears at first unstable exhibitionism in
Strindberg turns out on closer examination to be merely an exten-
sion and exaggeration of characteristically inconsistent Swedish
traits.

It is therefore not Strindberg's undoubted genius and range
alone which have made him his country's classic writer, the Swedish Dante, Goethe or Cervantes, and his *Master Olof* their *Hamlet*;
he makes their language sing and their minds stir. *The People of
Hemsö*, which to outsiders may appear to be not much more than a
bawdy rustic novel reminiscent of Rabelais and Zola but not as
good as either, is specifically named by Bergman as being one of
the Strindberg works which 'makes his hair stand on end'. He
cannot be alone in this, for the book has had huge sales in Sweden
and has been filmed there more than once. It is a folk-tale which
springs from the very fibres of the Swedish people. Its story of
canny peasants and fishermen, of pregnant brides and gargantuan
wedding-feasts, of the murderous winter tempests and the balmy
summer breezes blowing alternately over the archipelago which
every Swede invests with powerful erotic emotions – as innumer-

able films of the *Summer Interlude* variety attest – goes right to the
heart of the national consciousness. It is a consciousness which can
embrace the robust vulgar fun of Bergman's comedy or costume
movies, the black humour of a work like *The Face*, and the austere
probings of the painful 'serious' films, without any feeling of
contradiction. Swedish people seem more haunted than most by
the fear of death. Some of the finest cinematic moments in Bergman occur when jollity disintegrates suddenly into anguish, as at
the dinner-party in *A Passion*, or as in *The Seventh Seal* when the
sounds of junketing in the inn are faded off the sound-track and
this muttered conversation is amplified until it dominates the
scene:

> MERCHANT: Yes, it's true! The plague is spreading
> along the west coast. People are dying like flies.
> Usually business would be good at this time of year,
> but, damn it, I've still got my whole stock unsold.
> WOMAN: They speak of the judgement day. And all
> these omens are terrible. Worms, chopped-off hands
> and other monstrosities began pouring out of an old
> woman, and down in the village another woman
> gave birth to a calf's head.
> OLD MAN: The day of judgement. Imagine.
> FARMER: It hasn't rained here for a month. We'll
> surely lose our crops.
> MERCHANT: And people are acting crazy, I'd say.
> They flee the country and carry the plague with them
> wherever they go.
> OLD MAN: The day of judgement. Just think, just
> think!
> FARMER: If it's as they say, I suppose a person should
> look after his house and try to enjoy life as long as he
> can.
> WOMAN: But there have been other things too, such
> things that can't even be spoken of. (*Whispers*)
> Things that mustn't be named – but the priests say
> that the woman carries it between her legs and that's

why she must cleanse herself.

OLD MAN: Judgement day. And the Riders of the Apocalypse stand at the bend in the village road. I imagine they'll come on judgement night, at sundown.

WOMAN: There are many who have purged themselves with fire and died from it, but the priests say that it's better to die pure than to live for hell.

MERCHANT: This is the end, yes, it is. No one says it out loud, but all of us know that it's the end. And people are going mad from fear.

FARMER: So you're afraid too.

MERCHANT: Of course I'm afraid.

OLD MAN: The judgement day becomes night, and the angels descend and the graves open. It will be terrible to see. (*The Seventh Seal*, pp. 45-6)

The pictorial construction of many Bergman movies reflects this precarious balancing of divergent elements. There is a high degree of black-and-white contrast, and mood is accurately and swiftly revealed in facial expression. For example, in *The Seventh Seal* Mia and Jof, dressed in clown costumes, switch from extravagant gaiety as they perform their act to sobre disquiet as they contemplate the flagellants and the hell-fire preacher, the seriousness of the last image grotesquely reinforced by Jof's absurd cuckold's horns. Similarly in *Winter Light (Nattvardsgästerna)* the drabness of the weather and the shortness of the grey November day are reflected in the starkness of the images (whitewashed walls, black cassock) just as much as in the bleakness of the misery and solitude which the film exposes. The whole movie, in fact, orchestrates the central image so consistently that every element – even down to the pastor's influenza – comes together to make an overpowering statement about human dereliction. Strindberg similarly chose his climactic – and climatic – moments with care: *The Father* is set in midwinter, *Miss Julie* in midsummer. This fondness for extremes of weather, for the dichotomies of light and dark, makes possible and plausible the two artists' preoccupation with the meaning of life, with the problem of evil, and with the existence of God. 'Ever since childhood', Strindberg writes in *Inferno*, 'I have looked for God and found the devil', and the films of Bergman's middle period, especially *The Seventh Seal*, are concerned with precisely the same quest. 'What is going to happen to those of us who want to believe but aren't able to?' asks the Knight despairingly, but though 'he stops and waits for a reply, no one speaks or answers him'.

The problem of evil involves also the issue of sin, guilt and redemption. Strindberg had acute guilt complexes, particularly of an erotic kind; much as he practised (even by telepathy, as the extraordinary *Occult Diary* reveals) and enjoyed sexual intercourse, he seems never to have overcome a deep-seated disgust for it which poisoned relations with the women he courted and married. He was undoubtedly immature in this respect, for he could never resolve the conflict he felt between a desire, centred upon the one and same woman, to worship a virgin-mother figure and to defile a harlot-image. His rather puerile misogyny, which mars even his greatest works and led to the break-up of his marriages, must be traced to an inability to overcome his own conflicting attitudes to sexuality. There is no corresponding misogyny in Bergman's world: if anything, women are revealed as more sensitive and intelligent than their male counterparts. There is a no more telling indictment of male pusillanimity than the portrait of Jan in *Shame*, no more impressive a picture of female tenderness and forbearance than the figure of Alma in *Hour of the Wolf*. It is true that Strindberg's Daughter of Indra in *A Dream Play* shows a similar compassion, but it is of a rather generalized kind, and she is a symbolic figure rather than a woman of flesh and blood. It is true that there is some anxiety about sex in Bergman's movies. His couples do not always make a physical success of things; their torments can arise from personality clashes or temperamental difficulties (as in *Summer with Monika* (*Sommaren med Monika*), *Wild Strawberries*, or *Scenes from a Marriage* (*Scener ur ett äktenskap*)), from metaphysical anguish (as in *Winter Light*), or from mental illness (as in *Through a Glass Darkly* (*Såsom i en Spegel*)), but they do not usually arise from any Strindbergian preoccupation with sex as such (exceptions are characters like Ester in *The Silence* and David in *The Touch*, but they do not bear their creator's evident approval as they would be liable to do if they featured in a work by Strindberg). On the other hand, Bergman's characters do appear to suffer from a more generalized feeling of guilt over existence itself, at what Caldéron called 'el delito mayor del hombre', man's greatest offence, that is, the sin of having been born. As we might expect, the whole atmosphere of *The Silence* and *Shame* is redolent of an oppressive sense of guilt; guilt at living in this world at all, and guilt on the part of the artist for imagining such horrors:

> EVA: Sometimes everything seems like a long strange dream, it's someone else's, that I'm forced to take part in. Nothing is properly real. It's all made up. What do you think will happen when the person who has dreamed us wakes up and is ashamed of his dream? (pp. 145-6)

This is much more akin to the existential *angst* of the mid-twentieth century and especially to the stoicism of Beckett, reminiscent of Schopenhauer, than it is to the more personal torments of Strindberg, which smack of late Romanticism rather than the hard-headed modernism which pervades the work of Kafka's heirs. Here we meet with the distinction between Bergman as an 'objective exhibitioner' and Strindberg as a 'subjective exhibitionist'. Whereas most of Strindberg's conflicts can, indeed must, be traced to events in his own turbulent autobiography, relatively few of Bergman's intimately personal problems appear to seep too obtrusively through the filters of discretion which he has set up between his life and his work. In this reticence, of course, Bergman is more characteristically Swedish than Strindberg. He has hinted that some of his films – *Summer Interlude, Winter Light* and *Hour of the Wolf* in particular – are close to his heart 'for very personal reasons', but it is not possible (or necessary) to guess at what these reasons are. Strindberg, on the other hand, documented his private affairs in considerable detail, under only the thinnest of disguises – subterfuges which misled no one – such as the 'madman's defence' in which he told all (or at least a great deal, though largely of course from his own point of view) about his relations with Siri von Essen.

There are some obvious parallels between a few of Strindberg's plays and some of Bergman's films which are worthwhile to consider. The early film *Thirst (Törst)*, the more recent *A Passion* and *The Touch* have, inevitably in their treatment of triangular love relationships, something in common with Strindberg's discussion of the same theme in *Creditors* or in *The Dance of Death*: Kurt, the interloper in the second play, is sucked into a taut marriage situation in a claustrophobic island setting very like the one in which Bergman's Andreas Winkelman finds himself vis-à-vis Eva and Elis Vergérus. Likewise *The Seventh Seal*, with its medieval setting, episodic structure, 'stations' pattern, and 'static iconography of expressionist drama' recalls both historical plays by Strindberg like *The Saga of the Folkungs*, and visionary plays like *The Road to Damascus*. Similarly *The Stronger*, in which one of the two women characters is silent for the duration of the piece, presents, in this respect at least, an obvious analogy with *Persona*. But these are largely fortuitous coincidences of plotting which should not concern the critic overmuch.

We are on more solid ground in noting close similarities of mood between *Wild Strawberries* and *A Dream Play*: Peter Cowie quotes Bergman as saying 'Whenever I am in doubt and uncertainty I take refuge in the vision of a simple and pure love. I find this love in those spontaneous women who . . . are the incarnation of purity'. Though the remark sounds incongruous in Bergman's mouth, it is certainly characteristic of the Strindberg who created the Daughter of Indra in *A Dream Play* or Adèle in *The Ghost Sonata*. More significant still are the parallels between the dream interludes in *Wild Strawberries*, in particular the sequence in which the eminent scientist Isak Borg is ignominiously ploughed in a student examination and finds imposed on himself, as the penalty for failure, *ensamhet*: 'loneliness'. There is a similar nightmarish sequence in *A Dream Play*, where the Officer is sent back to school although he has long since graduated. In reply to his assertion that since once one is one, twice two must be two, the Schoolmaster replies, 'The proof is perfectly in accord with the laws of logic, but the answer is wrong', and he orders the Officer to remain at his desk for an indefinite period so that he may 'mature'. The difference between play and film, of course, is that in the play the School-master is a butt of ridicule, but in the film the examiner is terrifying. There is also a difference between the ceremony for the conferring of Doctors' degrees in *Wild Strawberries* and a similar one in *A Dream Play*. In the film, the festivities are merely boring, 'moments of refined torture' for Borg (though not for his friends and relatives, who are proud of his being thus honoured), whereas in the play they 'greatly agitate' the Lawyer since the Dancers refuse to crown him at the last moment.

Both play and film, of course, advance the notion of dream as a form of higher reality, of superior consciousness, and the play simply blurs the distinction to a greater extent. *Wild Strawberries* is suffused with the atmosphere of *A Dream Play*, since Bergman saw Molander's famous production at the impressionable age of sixteen and found it 'a fundamental dramatic experience'. But he has, for all that, produced a more schematic, neater, tougher, less self-indulgently whimsical work than Strindberg's, similar, perhaps, but not the same, and certainly not 'borrowed and edited Strind-berg'. Bergman's 'dream play' is less of a meditation on human suffering than a study in psychological renewal. But because it is ultimately a realistic story in a way that Strindberg's (being more of a parable) is not, it stands or falls by its plausibility in naturalistic terms. The motion picture – like the short story – is normally too brief in terms of duration of performance for it to be able to handle the kind of psychological odyssey which the more expansive novel form has made its own, but here an attempt is made. As it is, however, *Wild Strawberries* is not Bergman's greatest work, for it rubs too much against the grain of the medium. Notwithstanding its symbolic significance, Isak Borg's journey to Lund is too palpably a real journey, complete with stops to fill up with gasoline and to eat at a wayside restaurant, for it to become authentically Strindbergian.

There are fairly close parallels, too, between *Through a Glass Darkly*, the first and relatively optimistic film in Bergman's trilogy of investigations into faith and unbelief, and *Easter*, an uncharacteristically hopeful play from Strindberg's later years. In both works, the daughter's sickness at first casts a shadow over the family, and in both cases the illness is thought to be connected with spiritual insight. 'My illness is not sickness unto death', Strindberg's Eleanora declares, 'but unto the honour of God', and after her severest attack Bergman's Karin believes that she has seen God (albeit in the form of a loathsome spider, a twist Strindberg would not have considered very appropriate). In Bergman's film Karin accepts sacrifice that the others may be saved and reconciled to each other's faults and weaknesses. It is her reading of David's diary which pricks the bubble of his selfishness, and it is her act of incest with Minus that breaks through the boy's sexual claustrophobia. Through her sufferings the others learn a cardinal truth: 'God is love'. Less openly sentimental than *Easter*, Bergman's film nonetheless radiates (somewhat falsely) a faith and a sense of hope which is progressively undermined as the trilogy develops. But as it stands it tells, like Strindberg's play, of atonement, redemption, and renewal.

The last pair of works worthy of mention and comparison are *Miss Julie* and *Smiles of a Summer Night (Sommarnattens leende)*. By their respective authors' own admission the first is a tragedy, the second a romantic comedy (whether critics can accept the definition of *Miss Julie* as a tragedy is another matter; it reads best perhaps as black farce). Despite this cardinal difference, there are similarities. Both works are rooted in folklore: Strindberg dwells upon the pagan and magical associations of midsummer eve, and Bergman's film pivots around the traditional 'three smiles' a summer's night is supposed to show. Both works carry a marked erotic charge, but it is precisely here that the crucial distinction in sexual matters noted earlier is seen at its most evident. Love in *Miss Julie* is a besmirching weapon in the class and personality struggle, and betrays on the lovers' part a fundamental contempt for each other's sex, and the clash can have only one outcome, which is death. In Bergman's film sex is a celebration, enjoyed like a ritual dance, either the sophisticated minuet paced by the gentlefolk, or the boisterous jig pranced out by the serving people, in both cases an escape from the humdrum and the everyday, a leap into life and joy. Neither work is very plausible from a naturalistic point of view: Miss Julie's dialogue with Jean is not taut enough to be truly convincing, and her sexual surrender is too sudden to be credible; similarly, the neat way in which all turns out for the best in *Smiles of a Summer Night* is frank romantic fantasy. Strindberg's drama, however, has pretentions to naturalism, and its failure to match up to them is a weakness in the play's conception. Being less ambitious, Bergman's treatment of the same theme of summer madness is rather more successful.

Any parallels between Strindberg and Bergman clearly are not a crude result of slavish imitation by the latter of the former. If Strindbergian themes or situations are recalled, they are transmuted, sometimes completely, in Bergman's movies; for instance, a reference to Ibsen's *A Doll's House* (which the couple see in the second play of *Scenes from a Marriage*) points up the fact that Bergman is ironically setting his work in the Nordic tradition of tortured conjugal dramas. Both artists are enigmatic, symbolic, allusive rather than discursive, literal, explicit creators and both are relatively uninterested in technique *as such*. Strindberg was able to become a fundamental innovator in the history of drama because he expected the techniques of stage production to fall in with his conceptions, rather than the other way about. And Bergman rebuts the popular view that film, as an art form, is closest to literature. 'I would say', he writes, 'that there is no art form that has so much in common with film as music. Both affect our emotions directly, not via the intellect. And film is mainly rhythm; it is inhalation and exhalation in continuous sequence. Ever since childhood, music has been my great source of recreation and stimulation, and I often experience a film or play musically.' This might sound paradoxical coming from a cineast who is known for the intellectual content of many of his movies, and for the anguished metaphysical debate they conduct with the spectator. *The Silence* is painstakingly constructed of sequences of sharply differentiated quality, often cross-cut with some abruptness: the claustrophobic hotel suite alternates with the stifling street, for instance. The whole film has a musical patterning, a structure of moods which contrast subtly with each other. It is precisely this kind of alogical structure which Strindberg introduced into the writing of stage plays and which has had such a widespread influence on contemporary dramaturgy.

The two artists are in other ways less alike. Strindberg is diffuse and unfocused beside Bergman, whose works are disciplined and highly contrived. The crucial difference between the two, how-ever, is that in Bergman there is continuous debate – debate over the existence of God (in *The Seventh Seal* and *Winter Light*) and debate over the value of human life (in *Wild Strawberries* and *So Close to Life*). For Bergman, who is an agnostic yet still the son of a clergyman, the religious problem is of central importance and the 'result of this conflict is usually some kind of tower of Babel'. In Strindberg we miss this sort of rigorous debate, and we find instead an attitudinizing stance; he was even capable of projecting himself into the role of the alternately warm-hearted and savage, impuls-ive, violent, restless and half-crazy king Erik XIV. Thus even such indirectly autobiographical films as *The Face* and *Hour of the Wolf* are more ironical and complex than *A Madman's Defence* or *Inferno*. Where Strindberg goes in for self-pity, Bergman indulges in self-derision. Where Strindberg is a late Romantic, whose works can largely be taken at their face value, Bergman is a late Modern-ist, whose stances must be treated with some caution. This does not mean that Strindberg was incapable of detachment and self-scrutiny: a play like *The Father* or *The Dance of Death* is not an absolutely straight indictment of the woman in Strindberg's own life, and his portrait of the husband is not simple self-justification. Nuances exist, but so seldom that we are often near the naked souls – and not very attractive souls at that. This is not to dislike Strindberg for his opinions alone. It is possible, without contra-diction, to entertain reservations about T. S. Eliot's high toryism and greatly admire *The Waste Land*, because the politico-religious attitudes, though they underlie much in the poem, do not domi-nate it and still less exhaust its manifold meanings. It is equally possible to find Joyce's sexual fetishism distasteful and yet still to revere *Ulysses* which projects quite a lot of it. But if you do not care for Strindberg's paranoia, persecution mania and misogyny, it is rather difficult to admire unreservedly such works as *The Father* and *Miss Julie* which are suffused with them, not to speak of the more overtly self-revelatory books from *The Son of a Servant* onwards.

For all his achievements in stagecraft and dramaturgy which cannot be underrated, Strindberg was not a particularly subtle artist. He didn't lack humour – many of his writings are amusing to read – but he was totally without a sense of self-irony. He could not, like Kafka, have tittered with helpless laughter at the reading of his own horrendous tales; he could not, like Beckett thirty years on, have chuckled over the witticisms of his juvenilia. Strindberg ultimately took the world and himself too seriously. And that is why Ingmar Bergman, a more Shakespearian, or pehaps more Faustian figure, is fundamentally a more impressive creator than he. The most effective answer, therefore, to the jibe that Bergman is mere rehash of Strindberg is that he cannot be, since of the two he is no mere follower but, in respect of our world, the more accomplished artist.

Gothic and Grotesque

Hjalmar Bergman, the Swedish writer who lived from 1883 to 1931, is not particularly well known outside his own country, but within it his novels and plays are established classics of bitter-sweet comedy. In *Ingmar Bergman et ses films* Jean Béranger quotes Rune Waldekranz, the producer of Bergman's early masterpiece *Sawdust and Tinsel (Gycklarnas afton)*, as saying that Ingmar acquired his unique amalgam of humour and sarcasm from Hjalmar's comedies, which he knew well, not least from having produced two of his plays, *En Skugga (A Phantom)* and *Sagan (A Fairy-Tale)*, between 1950 and 1958. 'We have our own traditions', Bergman has said, and it is these which inspire so much of his work. The contact with Hjalmar is in the forefront of these. Frédéric Durand in his essay

'Ingmar Bergman et la littérature suédoise' argues that the cineast
owes to the playwright 'his bitter and provocative irrationalism',
and Jörn Donner has said that the two artists have in common 'the
same sense of the grotesque and the aberrant' (*The Personal Vision of
Ingmar Bergman*, p. 115). It is fair to conclude that the debt to
Hjalmar is most evident in the comic films and in the fatalistic
view of young love projected in the early movies. In his presentation of the translation of Hjalmar's *Four Plays* (Seattle: University
of Washington Press, 1968), Walter Johnson writes:

> Hjalmar Bergman's world is a moral world in the sense
> that he feels that there is a clear distinction between
> right and wrong, between good and evil . . . Bergman is
> basically pessimistic about the fate of Everyman in this
> imperfect world: the young, like Anne-Marie in *Mr
> Sleeman is Coming*, are essentially good and innocent,
> but they are helpless when confronted by evil in the
> form of the crippled, the apathetic, the bitter, and the
> powerful (pp. vi-vii).

In the narrow compass of a one-act expressionist play, Hjalmar
Bergman presents the Liebestod theme with a strong feeling for the
intensity of the erotic impulse, an impulse to destroy as well as to
create, which Strindberg explores in *Miss Julie*, Dreyer in *Day of
Wrath*, and Ingmar Bergman in *Hour of the Wolf*. But although
Hjalmar's pessimism and sense of the ultimate meaninglessness of
human life has much in common with Ingmar's, they are closest in
their attitude to comedy. Hjalmar's dialogue is pert and lively, and
like Ingmar he ironically undercuts his characters by giving them
outrageous things to say, as in this fragment from *Swedenhielms* in
which the Nobel prizewinner's children comically bemoan their
lot:

> JULIA: No, you can say what you want about theatre
>   people, but we have a sense of duty. I can, I will do
>   this part, even if I have to live at the dressmaker's.
>   But such is the life of a Swedish actress!
>   [*One of the charwomen enters with a bucket in one hand*

*and several letters in the other. She puts the letters on the
secretary and goes on to the windows.*]

ROLF [*walking back and forth*]: In Sweden the unwanted
child is, and always will be, the scientist. He doesn't
want to be discussed, and he seldom is. He seeks no
crass encouragement and as a result receives no
encouragement. He despises publicity, and the
public regards him as negligible at best. He loathes
the press, and the press covers his life's work in three
lines! So you see, Pedersen my boy, it isn't a bit
pleasant being a scientist in this country. [*He nearly
stumbles over the old woman's pail.*] Out of the way, you
old frump!

THE OLD WOMAN [*offended*]: It's no fun to be a
scrubwoman either.   (*Four Plays*, p. 198)

Both Bergmans display this acute perception of character beneath a
surface humour. Both show, too, a sharp sense of theatre: they both
know how best to use *coups de théâtre*, dramatic surprises, unexpected entries and exits. They differ, of course, in the excessive
stageyness of much of Hjalmar's writing, which is reminiscent
both of Giraudoux in its style and manner, and of Shaw in its
dramaturgy (the expository first scene is handled in a very Shavian
way). There are big, colourful characters, witty and richly orches-
trated dialogue, entrances often arranged to allow for audience
applause of their favourite actor or actresses. Hjalmar was, like
Ingmar, very much a professional, adapting his plays for radio and
films, and converting his successful novels (especially *Markurells i
Wadköping*, 1919) into stage and screen dramas. The rather
heavy-handed, folksy wit (such as 'there hasn't been a single affair
in this part of the country in the last fifty years that has escaped her
attention, whether it smelled of Chanel No. 5 or the haystack',
Four Plays, p. 154), very much designed with the pause for laughs
in mind is not at all like Ingmar's; even if it were, such methods are
really suitable only for the stage, although the Marx Brothers did
manage to perfect their use in films. But it is certainly not Ingmar's
way of doing comedy: his devices are more subtle, as we shall see.

In their works both artists are given to the slightly larger-than-life, and both are self-consciously Swedish, especially in their creation of characters; and in their awareness of latent menace they are very similar. In the work of both, threat and reprieve alternate: at the end of the play about the cuckold Markurell, one of Hjalmar's most characteristic creations, the hero accepts his role as a dupe, continues in his affection for his putative son and, somewhat in the manner of Isak Borg in *Wild Strawberries*, undergoes a radical change of heart from egotism to generosity: how typically Swedish that movie is can be seen by juxtaposing it with the rather incredible story of Markurell's redemption. The wheel comes full circle when we realize that Victor Sjöstrom (who plays Borg in Ingmar's film) based one of Sweden's first sound movies on Hjalmar's screen adaptation of his best-selling novel about the sly Markurell.

Nevertheless, helpful as it is to consider the two Bergmans side by side, it must be said that Hjalmar has not the artistic stature of Ingmar. To read him today is not only to discover a somewhat old-fashioned writer; it is also to experience a rather provincial one. In her introduction to the translation of *Markurells*, Stina Bergman tells how at the inauguration of the Hjalmar Bergman theatre in the author's home town of Örebro in 1965 'at least a hundred young people who had just finished their matriculation examinations asked to appear as unpaid extras in the last scene, in which the students come marching in with Johan at their head;' and she goes on, 'the old and yet eternally young Swedish student song, written by Prince Gustaf, poured out over the audience ...' (*Four Plays*, p. 8). All very jolly, no doubt; but her story indicates the essential limitations of Hjalmar Bergman as an artist. How different from this orgy of nostalgic sentiment, this aggressively provincial display of mawkish bonhomie, are Bergman's formally analogous but so much more profoundly moving sequences with the students in *Wild Strawberries*: when Marianne and Isak recite to them the words of Johan Olof Wallin's hymn, or when they wish the professor goodnight and young Sara, the image of Isak's lost love, tells him: 'Do you know that it is really you I love, today, tomorrow and forever?' To imagine a situation as supremely effective as this – even if it now appears dated and perhaps embarrassing

– was evidently beyond the workmanlike but limited talents of
Hjalmar Bergman. The scene owes much of its impact to the
expression on Sjöstrom's face: benign, sceptical but close to tears,
foreshadowing the movie's resolution.

If the robustness of Hjalmar's comic grotesque is one facet of
Ingmar's genius, the gothic world of several Scandinavian artists
represents another. Karen Blixen (Isak Dinesen), the Danish baro-
ness who wrote much of her *œuvre* in English, manifests this in
Seven Gothic Tales (1934); Lindsay Anderson was reminded of her in
watching *The Seventh Seal (Focus on The Seventh Seal*, p. 139). There
are even more striking parallels with the films of the Dane Carl
Dreyer (1889-1968). Bergman has refuted all imputation of direct
influence on him of Dreyer's style, and has ascribed any similarities
to their common Scandinavian background; he claims to dis-
approve of what he calls Dreyer's 'sado-masochistic attitude', his
'resignation', and above all the way in which he allegedly never
conceives 'a God for men' but only 'men for God' (Béranger,
p. 103). This sounds like protesting too much; Bergman is being
disingenuous if he is unable to see quite close similarities between
Dreyer's work and his own. Both cineasts are concerned with the
play of dark forces, with dramatic contrasts of light and shade,
both in the story and mise-en-scène; Bergman probably owes more
to Dreyer, in fact, than he cares to admit. Much of what Tom
Milne says about the typical Dreyer movie can apply, *mutatis
mutandis*, to Bergman's films also:

> The period is almost invariably the past. The subject is
> a small, self-enclosed group – a family, a village, a
> victim and her judges – with the action rarely moving
> outside an extremely restricted area, and rarely stretch-
> ing over more than a few hours or days; and within the
> group, a lonely figure gradually detaches itself, the
> object of either deliberate or unconscious cruelty. Styl-
> istically, there is a marked emphasis on close-up (actual
> in *La Passion de Jeanne d'Arc*, elsewhere more an impres-
> sion deriving from his closeness to his characters and
> insistence on his images); the solid presence of the

décor (a preference for real locations, or failing that, sets faithfully reconstructed in every detail even when, as in *Jeanne d'Arc*, only small segments would actually be used in any particular scene); soft-toned lighting, playing with a range of greys rather than high contrasts (even in a film of black-and-white juxtapositions like *Day of Wrath*); inexperienced actors, amateurs, worn old faces, all chosen for their presence (their 'mental resemblance', Dreyer has called it) and ability to merge with the atmosphere, setting and story, rather than for their proven acting ability. The tempo, above all, is a slow, stately cadence, vigorous but unhurried, and moving ineluctably towards the final catharsis of tragedy.

(*The Cinema of Carl Dreyer*, London 1971, pp. 25-6)

Two only of Milne's observations do not really apply to Bergman; one is the use of amateur actors; the other concerns the catharsis which ends a Dreyer film, but not a Bergman movie: in Bergman the endings are always more muted and ambiguous. But the films of the two cineasts are similar in texture (the high black-and-white contrasts of the scene of Anne's trial in *Day of Wrath* are very similar to those noted above in the mountebanks' sequence in *The Seventh Seal*), and in pace (both reveal a slow, deliberate manner); one notes in both styles the use of sharp camera angles and a fondness for close-up (especially facial and female, of the remarkable Falconetti in Dreyer's case and of Liv Ullmann in Bergman's), and for the communication of feelings by look and gesture, the camera itself underscoring the point by its concentration on a particular character at an especially eloquent moment. Moreover, there is perceptible in both directors a similarly intense atmosphere within a confined, even claustrophobic, world; strong sexual feelings, for instance, are conveyed obliquely by look, by husky, rather breathless voices (compare the surrender of Anne in *Day of Wrath*, with her half-whispered plea 'take me and make me happy', with Alma's 'tone of shameful lust' in the retelling of the episode of the beach in *Persona*). Both are psychological cineasts: 'so paramount is

the part played by psychology in Dreyer's films', writes Ole Storm
in his introduction to *Four Screenplays* (London 1970, p. 13), 'that
first and foremost his scripts emphasize the shifts of mood which
condition his characteristic camera rhythms'. So important is the
visual and cinematic portrayal of emotion to both cineasts that
Storm's point about Dreyer applies equally well to Bergman: 'The
dialogue is deliberately restricted. Only the barest minimum is
spoken. Everything essential is left to the camera' (p. 18). Both
directors practise what Dreyer describes as the following process:
'The audience must be made to forget that they are seeing a film,
and must be persuaded (or, if you prefer, hypnotized) into thinking
that they are witnessing a divine intervention, so that they may go
away gripped and silent' (p. 20). It is true that Bergman is departing from this mesmerism of his viewer in his later works; in *Hour of
the Wolf*, *Persona* and especially *A Passion* (with the clapper-board
introducing interviews with the actors) he breaks the illusion by
introducing the technical side – but only to plunge the audience
thereafter more firmly back into the drama.

   Both artists, too, operate best in a landscape. Bergman's island
setting of Fårö, his favoured location for some of his best movies,
plays, like Dreyer's Danish landscapes, 'an active part in the story
and releases feelings and perceptions beyond what can be expressed
on the stage' (Storm, p. 19). And both have an acute awareness of
the sordid cruelty of political machinations: Joan's 'utter despair
and loneliness' in Dreyer's *Passion of Joan of Arc* is paralleled by the
vulnerability of Jan and Eva in the interrogation centre in *Shame*. It
is true that there are differences over metaphysics: in Bergman we
have a feeling of the absence of God from his troubled world, in
Dreyer a brooding sense of sin, something Bergman is not greatly
bothered about, as we saw in the discussion of Strindberg earlier.
This difference is shown up in the different treatment meted out to
a son who seduces his father's young wife: in *Day of Wrath* the
penalty is a burning at the stake; in *Smiles of a Summer Night* a horse
and carriage is provided to bear the lovers away to happiness.

   But the difference is not so great as to diminish one's feeling that
Bergman and Dreyer have much in common. This is borne out if
one looks at individual works. *Vampire*, like *Hour of the Wolf*, is an

expressionist horror movie in the gothic tradition of *Nosferatu* and *The Cabinet of Doctor Caligari*; and the similarities of iconography with the classics of this early movement indicate parallels between *Vampire* and the dream sequences in *Wild Strawberries*; both films have a 'two men for one coffin' motif (see *Four Screenplays*, p. 117, for the phrase 'in bewilderment he bends over his own corpse', and compare it with 'to my horror, I saw that the corpse was myself' in *Wild Strawberries*, p. 27); and in *Vampire* the ego of the hero is divided as in *Persona* and *Hour of the Wolf*. There is a similar contrast between normality and strangeness, a common feeling that nothing and everything is real, in *Vampire* and in *A Passion*. What takes place within the domestic setting is fantastic, and, as the action develops, gradually becomes 'unaccountable to reason, absurd and evil', writes Ole Storm of Dreyer's film (p. 15), but his words could describe *Hour of the Wolf* with equal aptness.

There is a notable similarity on a technical level between Dreyer's *The Word* and *The Seventh Seal*: in his hallucination Johannes sees the sweeping headlights of the doctor's car as the scythe of the hourglass man coming to bear Inger off into death; likewise in *Through a Glass Darkly* Karen assimilates the arrival of the helicopter seen through the window with the giant insect which she believes is attempting to rape her. And like Bergman's anguished Knight, Dreyer's Mikkel rages against the 'meaninglessness' of a world in which all that he has loved and worshipped is about to be clamped down in the earth 'to *rot* ... yes, *rot* ...' (*Four Screenplays*, p. 287). There is a happy ending, miraculous or unnatural according to one's point of view; a debate is going on in the film, however, similar to the sort of argument Bergman conducts with himself: in this case, concerning the triumph of good over evil.

Though there are numerous similiarities in the work of Dreyer and Bergman, these may largely be a result of their common background. By birth and upbringing they share outlooks and attitudes which to the foreigner may appear remarkably similar, but it does not appear that Bergman was consciously influenced by Dreyer, to whose quietism and acceptance of human suffering he objected. Dreyer is the author of at least one cinematic masterpiece, *Joan of Arc,* one of the classics of the silent film. The rest of his work, with the exception of *Day of Wrath,* is not of the same quality; and indeed his total production is limited to fourteen feature films (the majority silent) and a handful of shorts. He certainly cannot rank with Bergman either in range or in depth; but what he has left is impressive, and especially instructive when set alongside Bergman's achievement.

CHAPTER TWO

EARLY FILMS

The emotional and intellectual impact of Bergman's more mature work tends understandably to overshadow the films made early in his career, which risk being accorded a lesser importance in relation to his career as a whole than they perhaps deserve. Already the early films deal principally with forms of isolation, with a sense of oppression, often with humiliation and invariably with an element of despair. *Journey into Autumn (Kvinnodröm)* and *A Lesson in Love (En lektion i Kärlek)* stand out as ending 'happily' in that the protagonists overcome their troublesome situations, but in each case this is something of a dramatic illusion. The structure of *Journey into Autumn,* with almost identical opening and closing scenes, suggests a negation of grief rather than an acceptance of happiness; behind the superficial coyness of the ending of *A Lesson in Love* is the knowledge that both the Ernemans have had to abdicate part of their right to individual expression in order to renew their life together. They are merely entering a new phase in their continuing struggle, giving little cause for hope beyond mere survival in the later phases.

The earliest of Bergman's films deal particularly with a search for an independent relationship with the world at large. This is a typical and perennial difficulty for the adolescent, but also for the artist, whose problems loom large in Bergman's major work. The conviction that hell is on earth and its tortures by no means restricted to the hereafter also permeates the early films.

A number of familiar Bergman traits are present in his first cinematic venture, *Frenzy* (1944), for which he wrote the script and worked as assistant director to Alf Sjöberg. Usually taken as Bergman's first film, Jörn Donner suggests that it remains 'an important picture as Bergman's film, not Sjöbergs' (*The Personal Vision of Ingmar Bergman,* p. 32). *Frenzy* deals somewhat unsubtly with a complex of relationships between oppressors and victims. The central character is Jan-Erik, a romantic, idealistic boy from a middle-class home, in his last year at school. Meeting Bertha drunk in the street, he takes her to her flat, where she is fearfully expecting a visit from a mysterious man who later turns out to be Caligula, a sadistic schoolmaster who persecutes Jan-Erik in class. Jan-Erik has an affair with Bertha, but one day finds her dead on her bed with Caligula outside the flat. Caligula is not her murderer; the police release him after establishing that Bertha died of a heart attack. Expelled from school, after Caligula denounces him to the headmaster, Jan-Erik moves into Bertha's flat after confronting his father. The headmaster visits him, commiserates with him and gives him money: Jan-Erik faces life again.

Jan-Erik and Bertha are both victims and prisoners: Jan-Erik of home, school, Caligula, youthfulness and inexperience; Bertha of her situation, Caligula, life in general. The social background of the film is the Swedish middle class, with all its respectable connotations, so that in one sense all the characters in the film are its prisoners, and Jan-Erik's search for escape from his situation is a revolt against what society demands of him. Like Tomas' flight with Birgitta-Carolina in *Prison,* or Harri and Monika's escape to the Stockholm skerries in *Summer with Monika,* Jan-Erik's affair with Bertha is a romantic grasping at momentary happiness, and is equally ineffective, except as a step on his way to adulthood. Robin Wood points out the element of wish-fulfilment in the film, in that Jan-Erik eventually comes out on top, walking out on his father, and ignoring Caligula's pleas for help and understanding as he leaves Bertha's flat for the next phase of his life. It is tempting to suppose that Bergman expresses through Jan-Erik some of his own adolescent feelings (Jörn Donner recalls that the original idea for the script came to Bergman in his last year at school); the view of individual revolt against society, however, is broader than Bergman's own experience, and the film does contain an important insight, that oppressors themselves may be victims. Caligula in particular is a victim of his own malevolent impulses, like the child-murderer in Lang's *M*, and is at least a pitiably human if thoroughly unsympathetic figure.

Crisis (1945), from the play *Moderdyret* by the Danish author Leck Fischer, was the first film directed by Bergman. Yet, perhaps because the script was not his own, *Crisis* seems less of a Bergman film than *Frenzy*. Bergman dismisses it as 'lousy through and through' (*Bergman on Bergman,* p. 22), but the central character of Jack, which Bergman introduced into the play, is recognizably in the Bergman mould. Self-centred and unable to come to grips with reality, he ends by committing suicide in defiance of the taunts of his mistress. Jörn Donner (p. 20) describes Jack as 'a living dead man', adding that 'such figures of pain and suffering we shall often meet again', while the contrast between Jenny and her foster-daughter Ingeborg reflects the typical conflict between youth and age. The film also foreshadows the presence of Death as a character in its own right; Ingeborg is terminally ill – a developing feature in Bergman's later work – and her relationship with Jenny is reminiscent of the Anna-Ester relationship in *The Silence.*

Before *Prison* Bergman made no films from his original scripts, although two films from this period (apart from *Frenzy*) were made from his scripts by Gustav Molander, and are more recognizably Bergmanesque than those he himself directed. These were *Woman without a Face (Kvinna utan ansikte)* (1947) and *Eva (Eva)* (1948), which had its premiere after *Port of Call (Hamnstad)*, a fair example of Bergman's direction in this period. *Crisis* and subsequent films were affected by the mood of late 'thirties French cinema, in particular the work of Marcel Carné, whose influence (*Quai des Brumes* comes especially to mind) is traceable in the mood and setting of *Port of Call*. A much stronger influence, however, is that of post-war Italian neo-realism, specifically the work of Rossellini. Bergman admits that at this stage he was still searching for a personal style; even so, *Port of Call* is more than mere pastiche. The neo-realist manner suits the circumstances of the rather drab story, and balances the unrealistically romantic attitudes of both Gösta and Berit. Underlying the film is conflict with authority, represented both by Berit's mother and by the social worker responsible for Berit, on probation after a term in approved school.

Berit is a victim of the State system and of her parents' failed marriage; having arranged an abortion for her friend Gertrud, she can only avoid being sent back to approved school by divulging the name of the abortionist, betraying not only Gertrud but all the girls of their class whose only means of ending an unwanted pregnancy is the back-street practitioner. Gösta is bewildered and indecisive, escaping like Berit from the reality of life into the make-believe world of romantic love, a fantasy which does not stand up either to his discovery that Berit has been in an approved school or to his involuntary involvement in the aftermath of Gertrud's abortion. In a desperate evasion of their responsibilities they plan to run away, even arranging a passage on a cargo boat, but realizing the futility of their flight turn back at the last moment to continue in Sweden their struggle against life. The film ends on a rising note, with a romantic long shot of the two walking on a hill above Gothenburg, and with the hopefulness of Berit's final speech: 'It will soon be summer'. While neither Gösta nor Berit could hope to survive alone, together they have a chance.

Set in bleak mid-winter, *Prison* (1949) is the first film that Bergman directed from his own original script; the ideas which the film works out are no longer qualified by another director's style or limited by a script based on someone else's work. It is also his first overt attempt to come to grips with the paradoxical prevalence of evil and suffering in a society ostensibly based on a religion of love. Bergman sums up the basis of the film: 'What is her guilt, that she has to live this nauseating life? ... Why do we stand so foolishly powerless against evil ... Is earth hell, and is there in that case also a God, and where is he?' (quoted in Donner, p. 56), and: 'For me, hell has always been a most suggestive sort of place, but I've never regarded it as being anywhere else than on earth. Hell is created by human beings on earth. What I believed in in those days ... was the existence of a virulent evil, in no way dependent upon environmental or hereditary factors' (*Bergman on Bergman*, p. 40). In modern Swedish literature this notion is most obvious in Strindberg, but it is also a conscious attempt in the medium of film to emulate the nihilism and apocalyptic despair of the 'fyrtiotal' (i.e. 1940's) school of Swedish literature.

Structurally, the film is a play within a play, the story of
Birgitta-Carolina running parallel to the background of the film
studio scenes, the two linked by Tomas. Inclusion of silent film
and dream sequences adds a further dimension. Bergman mixes
naturalistic detail with expressionistic composition, plus an occasional touch of neo-realism (for instance, in the film studio
sequences); he contrasts and balances the starkness of real life with
the romanticism of the film world; Birgitta-Carolina's inexorable
defeat with Tomas' truce with circumstance.

A long pre-title sequence introduces the external framework; an
old man walks down a narrow road in a bare landscape. He is
Martin's old mathematics teacher, recently released from a mental
hospital, on his way to Martin's film studio to suggest that Martin
should make a film about hell and the pre-eminence of the Devil in
the world. Martin derides the idea but later relates the incident to
Tomas, a writer of the 'fyrtiotal' school, and his wife Sofi. Tomas
suggests that an article he based on an interview with a prostitute
might serve as the basis for such a film; a flashback to the interview
introduces us to Birgitta-Carolina. She is certainly more in control
of that situation than the nervous and uncertain Tomas, who
appears to be quite out of his depth and unable to comprehend her
casual acceptance of her way of life. At this point Bergman cuts to a
shot of a Stockholm street and the titles roll, beginning *Prison*
proper, the 'suggested' film based on the old man's idea.

It is winter, some six months after the interview. Birgitta-
Carolina, in obvious physical distress, makes her way along the
street and up a flight of stairs to the flat she shares with Peter, her
fiancé/pimp and Linnea, his sister. In the flat she gives birth to a
baby, which Peter and Linnea say they will 'take care of';
Birgitta-Carolina necessarily resigns herself to the implication that
they will kill it. This first act of victimization of Birgitta-Carolina
introduces the major figures of oppression in the film; Robin
Wood points out the function of Peter and Linnea as parental
authorities and the potential for exploitation implicit in the
pimp-whore relationship extends this situation beyond a simple
generation conflict. Peter's victimization of Birgitta-Carolina is
doubly significant when it becomes clear that Linnea dominates

him. This is the first occurrence of the emotionally stronger woman in a relationship (for other instances, compare Jan and Eva in *Shame*, Alma and Johan in *Hour of the Wolf*). Another repressive influence on Birgitta-Carolina takes the form of two police officers, who come to the flat to check on her; driven by guilt at the thought of the murdered baby, she makes the first of her three flights to hide in the basement − a dark, oppressive prison, with barred windows. Here she meets a small boy (escaping from his mother) who shows her the hiding place for his hunting-knife.

Meanwhile Tomas, drunk and despairing of the state of his marriage, decides that the only solution is the double suicide of himself and Sofi; Sofi knocks him out with a bottle and leaves him unconscious − on coming to, convinced that he has murdered her, he brings a policeman to the flat where there is, of course, no *corpus delicti*. Sitting bewildered in the street, Tomas meets Peter and Birgitta-Carolina on their way back from the police station where Peter has managed to convince the police that Birgitta-Carolina does not deserve their attention. Birgitta-Carolina and Tomas recognize each other; when Peter leaves them to get matches for Tomas' cigarette, they run and take refuge in the attic room of a boarding house. Here they are temporarily safe, free from external influence and able to believe themselves happy and hopeful. Their sense of security in the womb-like attic increases with a regression into childhood − among the impedimenta stored in the room Tomas finds an old projector and shows a film. This is in part a personal indulgence by Bergman, who in his own childhood used to run early silent films through his own primitive projector. It is also important within the movie, since the film (not, in fact, an actual film but a reconstructed pastiche acted by an Italian mime company; bits of it reappear in the opening sequence of *Persona*) summarizes the underlying theme of *Prison*, at the same time offering a parallel to Birgitta-Carolina's life and the human condition in general. It depicts a man in bed awakened by the entry of a burglar, who chases him with a club; the man attempts to hide in a chest, from which arises an enormous spider, and then in a cupboard from which appears a skeleton (Death). On the arrival of a policeman the whole thing develops into a circular chase round the room ending with Death pursuing all three out of the window.

Birgitta-Carolina falls asleep, into a dream also related to the action of the film. Wandering through a mist, she comes across a number of dark-clad people, all of whom turn their backs on her. She meets a girl, also dressed in black (Death again?), refusing her offer of a diamond. She approaches a man she thinks is Tomas, but when he turns round the face is a mask (a hint of *Wild Strawberries, The Face* and *Persona*). She sees a doll floating in a tub of water (her drowned baby); a pair of masculine hands picks it up, whereupon it turns into a fish which the hands kill by twisting its neck. The dream foreshadows her own death, emphasizing her isolation and vulnerability while suggesting that Tomas is not after all able to provide her with a way out. The point is repeated again the following morning, when Birgitta-Carolina witnesses a scene in the boarding house between a girl and her lover, a postman. She tells him she is pregnant – he reacts delightedly and they begin to plan their marriage. This is in sharp contrast to the outcome of Birgitta-Carolina's own pregnancy (Peter is also a Post Office employee); whereas the girl is full of joy, she has been singled out for unhappiness. She returns in despair to Linnea and Peter, who bring one of her former clients to the flat, intending her old life to resume where it left off. Clearly frightened, she refuses the man; Peter and Linnea, who know him to have sadistic tendencies, cynically leave her to him. He burns her with his cigarette; she flees for the last time to the basement, where she uses the boy's hunting-knife to kill herself. When she dies, she lies in a single shaft of light coming through the barred window, light which Jörn Donner (p. 64) calls 'light of mysticism, a light of grace and mercy'. She is finally at peace but her suffering in the first place remains unexplained. Tomas, meanwhile, returns home to the unmurdered Sofi and they decide to try again to reconstruct their marriage. The end of the film brings us back to the original framework for Birgitta-Carolina's story, with the teacher returning to ask Martin's opinion of the idea. Martin tells him that such a story would be impossible to film, because it would have to end in an unresolved question (as Birgitta-Carolina's story does) which only God, assuming he exists, could answer. The irony is that the film *has* been made, the 'unresolved question' its very point.

Prison is important in drawing together motifs discernible in previous films, making them into a platform on which Bergman bases his subsequent handling of those motifs. It is not a polished or subtle movie (shot in less than three weeks) but does establish the investigation of individual anguish as Bergman's prime concern and indicates the beginning of his own distinctive cinematic style.

Thirst (1949) already marks considerable development of that style. In contrast to previous films, Bergman for the first time presents mature characters with some experience of life. It is also the first of his many films in which the female point of view is central. The film (like *The Silence* and *Persona*) deals with the possibility of two women as aspects of a single character. The Rut-Bertil relationship extends the Sofi-Tomas relationship in *Prison*, while Viola is a polished reiteration of Birgitta-Carolina. As Rut and Bertil travel home to Sweden from Basle, Viola travels mentally to her death; the two strands of the plot do not come together but connect through Viola's meeting with Rut's friend Valborg. A desperate claustrophobia characterizes the Rut-Bertil relationship, intensified by scenes between them all taking place in a hotel room or railway carriage. As in *The Silence*, there is a feeling of isolation from the world, as much an encapsulation of their bodies in the carapace of the railway compartment as of their personalities in the tight circle of their own egotism. A graphic example of this point is the scene where Bertil and Rut are eating in the train when it stops at a German station and starving children appear at the window begging for food (the film is set in the immediate post-war period); Bertil makes a comment about Germans being too busy satisfying their hunger to concern themselves with introspection. Their spiritual sterility balances Rut's physical sterility – she has had a presumably inexpert abortion – and the gaping hole at the centre of their marriage. They stay together because as so often for Bergman's couples, hell shared is preferable to hell alone; the sequences dealing with Viola show the results of the latter. Her loneliness is mentally unbalancing her. Both a psychiatrist and Valborg, from whom she seeks help, prey on her, trying to abuse her for their own physical gratification. She commits suicide, her walk to the water to drown herself reproducing almost exactly the set, vacant expression and round-shouldered resignation of Berit engaged on the same errand at the opening of *Port of Call*.

Bertil (together with Tomas, of whom he is a development) is an early example of the artist's difficult reconciliation of personal and public sides of his art, a problem which Bergman investigates more particularly in *To Joy (Till glädje)* (1949) which centres on the break-up of the marriage between Stig and Martha due to Stig's musical ambitions. Again the seasons complement Bergman's situation – here summer is a background symbol of happiness, a device already used in *It Rains on our Love (Det regnar på vår kärlek)* and in flashback in *Thirst*, and destined to play an important role in the next group of films.

In *Summer Interlude* (1950), summer – and the Stockholm archipelago with which it is often associated in Bergman's work – forms the backdrop to an idyllic first love affair between Marie and Henrik. The film shows Marie's approach to spiritual and emotional maturity through her painful acceptance of the memory of that ultimately tragic affair.

The film opens in the Stockholm Opera, where Marie – now a ballet dancer within sight of the end of her career – is dancing in *Swan Lake*. Receiving Henrik's diary from her Uncle Erland, who had stolen it at the time of the affair, she returns to the island where it all happened. The flashback to the fateful summer is sharply contrasted by the present autumnal chill, just as the carefree youthfulness of the two lovers is contrasted with the more sober adult figures: Henrik's aunt – who appears in the 'present' as a small, black-clad figure (like the woman in *Face to Face* a presentiment and personification of death) – and Uncle Erland, a sinister blend of quasi-parental authority and menacing sexuality already familiar from earlier films. Erland's malice is evident in sending Marie the diary, expecting it to cause her pain by re-opening an old wound. In the flashback sequences, Marie and Henrik go through all the delightful experiences of first love; wild strawberries make their first appearance as a potent symbol of youthful happiness. All is perfect until Henrik's accidental death; not a simple and quick death — the camera concentrates on the whole of his last pain-racked minutes (he dives into the water, strikes a rock and tries to climb back up the bank before finally collapsing). Marie sub-sequently uses her career as a defensive wall against the realities she does not want to face, hardening her personality accordingly. There is contrast between the parity of her relationship with Henrik and the sordidness of Erland's desire for her. Erland, evil though he is, nevertheless invites compassion, since we learn that he has been embittered by an unrequited love for Marie's mother in his own youth. When Marie meets him at the villa in the 'present' she is able to exorcise his malevolent influence on her, just as she has been able to absorb the pain of the affair with Henrik. On her return to the Opera House ballet, we see her finally at one with her former refuge, the formalized world of her art. By inviting David, her current boy friend, to read Henrik's diary she offers one indication of her liberation from the past.

Although questioning God's existence in a world in which Marie's unhappiness is all too frequent, *Summer Interlude* is a relatively optimistic film. Technically it is extremely accomplished, using with considerable effectiveness devices which tend to the commonplace in later films. There is the characteristic Fischer lighting of the face, for instance: concentrating strongly on one side, leaving the other in darkness. There is the expressionistic use of cloud, too; a dark cumulus is seen behind Erland's head as he proposes to the young Marie, and a vertical pan reveals a similarly threatening cloud hovering over Henrik as he writhes in pain after his fatal dive. Crows caw, sudden gusts of wind toss the treetops, figures are silhouetted against the skyline, and the soundtrack fades into silence as if to emphasize the awesomeness of an impending utterance and lift it out of time. The ballet setting allows stress — as in *Sawdust and Tinsel* and *The Face* — on stage make-up; the face of the dancer playing Coppelius the magician is clownlike, twisted in the grimace of tragicomedy. When Marie wipes off her grease-paint in the closing sequence and pulls off her false eyelashes the gestures serve to emphasize her return to the 'present' with a new acceptance. A strikingly mature film, therefore, in which the

potential banality of the cliché about summer in the archipelago is
turned to good account.

Summer also forms the background to *Waiting Women (Kvinnors
väntan)* (1952), in which four women sitting together in a summer
cottage awaiting the return of their husbands relate episodes
of stories within stories, presented in flashback, expressing the
familiar philosophy that hell together is better than hell alone. It is
interesting, however, with regard to subsequent films. The sparse
dialogue of the second episode looks forward to *The Silence*, while
the final episode, in which the young sister of one of the principal
characters escapes in a boat with her boy friend, invites immediate
comparison with *Summer with Monika*. More important, though, is
the episode in which Karin and Frederick Lobelius (played by Eva
Dahlbeck and Gunnar Björnstrand) are stuck in a lift, the evident
potential of that collaboration leading directly to *A Lesson in Love*.

In *Summer with Monika* (1952) Bergman returns to the youthful
revolt and lower class background of his pre-*Thirst* films. Both
Monika and Harri are fed up and frustrated; Monika works in a
wholesale greengrocer's, Harri as junior assistant in a china-and-
glass warehouse. Monika comes from a family living in a small,
sordid tenement flat, where there is neither peace nor privacy.
Harri – his mother dead, his father remote – is the only son of a
lower middle-class family, in which looms an awesome but benevolent elderly aunt. Both are victims of their workplaces: Harri is
clumsy and inefficient, Monika is the only girl in the store, and
attractive too. Of the two, Monika is the stronger personality,
though her view of life outside her immediate environment is
understandably unrealistic (witness the cinema scene with her in
tears over a slushy romance). Their flight together in Harri's
father's boat is both a quest for their own identities and a defiance
of the world they hate; the journey in bright sunlight through the
waterways of Stockholm and out to the islands is full of youthful
exuberance and optimism. Their summer together is idyllic,
almost orgiastic. Even the appearance of Lelle, an ex-boy friend of
Monika who has already beaten up Harri once out of jealousy and
now sets fire to the boat, provides Harri with the opportunity to
assert his new-found manhood by beating him in a fight which is a

virtual parody of all Hollywood slugging matches. It is impossible to take the fight seriously, though its occurrence is important in view of Monika's later unfaithfulness with Lelle. As autumn approaches, however, the idyll comes to an end; short of food, with Monika pregnant, they decide to return to the city. The return journey, in a choppy sea, into a lowering sky, is in sharp contrast to their summer life. Harri accepts adult responsibility whereas Monika resents it; her life as the wife of an engineering apprentice fails to provide her with the excitement and entertainment she wants. With Harri away on a business trip, she takes up with Lelle again, going out to drink, dance and have a good time. A notable long shot in this sequence shows Monika looking straight into the camera with a partly contemptuous, partly defiant expression. Harri returns earlier than expected and sees Lelle leaving the tenement; in the subsequent scene Monika tells Harri that it is as much his fault as hers that their marriage has failed, because he has spent more time on his engineering studies than in caring for her. They are incompatible, but unlike Rut and Bertil in *Thirst*, they divorce and go their separate ways. Monika disappears to an unknown fate (implying another whore/victim like Birgitta-Carolina), leaving Harri literally holding the baby; at the end of the film he walks off behind his aunt, the child in his arms, back to his old home and towards the problems of maturity.

Behind *Summer with Monika* is the question of the validity of the dream and its total disappearance in the face of reality. Because of her inability to come to terms with an empty fantasy, there is an exasperating naivety about Monika. Her defeat is the more tragic because she was the prime mover in the original flight. The message 'compromise or die' is clear enough, but against the possibilities of that summer, compromise is poor reward.

Bergman says that *Summer with Monika* marks the end of his 'spotty-faced period' (*Bergman on Bergman*, p. 79). Henceforth his movies develop a harder edge, taking on a desperately introspective quality characteristic of the films from the late 1950's onwards. It marks, clearly, the end of the 'early' period – the next film, *Sawdust and Tinsel (Gycklarnas afton)* (1953), belongs quite definitely to his mature works, showing considerable dramatic and technical development. Between it and *The Seventh Seal* (1956), however, come three films which can be seen as bridging the gap between two distinct phases in Bergman's career. They have a certain continuity in that Gunnar Björnstrand, Eva Dahlbeck and Harriet Andersson play major parts in all three. A voice over the opening titles describes the first, *A Lesson in Love* (1954), as 'a comedy which might have been a tragedy'; it is actually an extremely amusing film, its humour ranging from the delicately extended situation joke in the railway carriage to the pure slapstick of the wedding sequence, all underpinned by reminders that beneath the surface life is rather less amusing.

The film opens with a confrontation between Erneman, a gynaecologist, and his mistress Susanne, whom he is trying to discard, on the grounds that he is too old and tired for such a liaison. Having taken up with her in the first place as an assertion of his youth and virility, he now wishes to retreat to his real self. He jumps on a train to Malmö; on the journey a photograph of his daughter Nix falls out of his book, setting off a flashback which explores the father-daughter relationship. Nix – reflecting perhaps a development of youthful protest in earlier films – does not want to be a girl; she hates being forced into a feminine mould, wears masculine clothes as often as possible, despises her friends' amorous adventures with boys. Anxious that achievement will elude her on account of her sex, she wants to create things with her hands, make a mark on the world. Erneman promises an apprenticeship with her uncle, a potter, solving her immediate problem but not the problem of his real inability to improve their relationship.

In the train a hilarious scene revolves around a bet between Erneman and a commercial traveller as to who will be the first to kiss a certain woman in their compartment. Erneman wins, the woman turning out to be his wife Marianne. She is also heading for Malmö, to join Carl-Adam, her lover and ex-fiancé, on his trip to Copenhagen. Carl-Adam and Erneman were once close friends – a flashback revealing that Erneman and Marianne had married after she had failed to show up at the ceremony in which she was to have been married to Carl-Adam. The scene where the wedding ceremony degenerates into a free-for-all is genuinely funny, but one

feels all the time that Erneman comes off best in ending up married
to Marianne. Another flashback, to Erneman's father's birthday
the previous summer, puts the marriage in perspective. His
mother treats her husband like a child; he is the centre of an
elaborate waking-up and present-giving on the morning of his
birthday, and as the family is about to set out for a picnic he is sent
back from the car to put on long underwear. Marianne sums it up
in one speech on the train: 'A mature grown man is a rarity, so one
has to find the child who suits one best'. Erneman accompanies
Marianne and Carl-Adam to Copenhagen, where he and Carl-
Adam get atrociously but hilariously drunk; a fight breaks out.
Marianne and Erneman escape in the subsequent confusion to be
met by Sam, Erneman's chauffeur, at which point it becomes clear
that Erneman has foreseen, directed and timed to the split second
the whole course of events. They go to a hotel room, ready-booked
with champagne waiting. The film ends in a mannered style with a
Cupid toddling along the corridor to hang a 'Do not disturb' notice
on their door.

Although Bergman says that *A Lesson in Love* was 'only made for
the passing moment' (*Bergman on Bergman*, p. 79) it does not
deserve dismissal as a lightweight film. Robin Wood (p. 62 et seq.)
thinks it is 'under-estimated and neglected' although he holds
reservations about its structure, reflecting his admitted difficulty
in distinguishing the outer frame from the flashbacks. The story is
coherent and the flashbacks appropriate once one realizes that the
frame of the film is the journey beginning in Erneman's consulting
room and ending in the Copenhagen bar. The important thing
about Bergman's humour is that it is based on compassion.
Beneath the comedy are the familiar themes of the necessary
compromise in human relationships and limitations to the search
for happiness and individual fulfilment, expressed in three generations of the Erneman family. Finally, as *A Lesson in Love* evolved out
of an episode in *Waiting Women*, we can discern in it the seeds of
other films. The Erneman-Nix relationship is the forerunner of
that between father and daughter in *Through a Glass Darkly* and in
a number of ways (the journey motif, the layered family relationships, even Erneman senior as a light sketch for Isak Borg) the film

looks forward to *Wild Strawberries.*

Journey into Autumn (1955) juxtaposes the dreams of two women (*Kvinnodröm*, 'woman's dream'). Susanne, a successful fashion photographer, obsessed with the desire to resume her affair with Henrik, a Gothenburg businessman, arranges a photo session there in order to see him. She takes one of her models, Doris, with her. Doris is reluctant to go as her boy friend Palle has just passed his matriculation examination; because her sudden departure for Gothenburg prevents the celebration he has planned, a row ensues between them. Doris is an empty-headed romantic — Monika with a more glamourous job; like her, one supposes, she dreams of immediate luxury. Tormented by her love for Henrik, Susanne contemplates suicide in a harrowing sequence on the train, Bergman cutting from shots of her face to the door of the train, focusing on the handle, the 'Open' and 'Shut' signs, and the warning notice about the danger of unlocked doors. She is prepared for any form of humiliation in order to get Henrik back — watching his house, using the telephone in a tea shop to try embarrassingly to persuade him to visit her hotel room. When he does, it is to relate his own humiliation — his business is failing, he needs his wife's money in order to survive, and lacks the courage to risk leaving her. Nonetheless, overcome by their feelings they go to bed. Henrik's wife duly arrives to confront them; freshly humiliated, he leaves with her, then returns merely to collect his briefcase, shattering Susanne's momentary joy.

Meanwhile, Doris has been window-shopping, dreaming girlishly of owning the fine clothes and jewellery on display. Bergman uses an interesting technique, shooting the whole sequence, including the appearance of Consul Sönderby, as a reflection in the shop window; Sönderby's face materializes like some genie of the lamp over Doris' shoulder. Together they act out their respective fantasies, Doris revelling in the dream-come-true of having the admired goods bought for her, Sönderby attempting to recapture something of his youth, a fleeting happiness in what later is shown to be his decidedly sad life. In an amusement park he suffers the torture of the switch-back and ghost train; in this sequence he is a straight-forward victim, a point reinforced by the direct relationship of the ghost train to the silent film pastiche in *Prison*. On leaving the park he collapses, his isolation emphasized by a high-angle long shot where the only people in the frame are himself and Doris, whose help he refuses. The maintenance of his urbane, dignified façade is all-important to him; it is the mask behind which he hides his real torment. At his house, in an atmosphere of wistful and unfulfillable sexuality, Doris dresses in her new finery; they dance and drink champagne. Doris reveals her empty and selfish aims, concerned entirely with her own looks and the possibility of fame. Her suggestion that Sönderby's money should finance her ambitions reminds him of his solitude; he has made no personal contact with the girl, who only sees him as a means to an end. His daughter, a habitual and embittered alcoholic, arrives to demand money, eventually blackmailing him on discovering Doris in a side room. A personal guilt complex surrounds these three: the now broken relationship between Sönderby and his fantasy daughter (Doris) highlights the completely broken-down relationship between Sönderby and his real daughter, intensified by the fact that his daughter bears a close resemblance – visible in a portrait – to her mother, inmate of a mental asylum for the last twenty-three years. This is the root of the isolation behind Sönderby's desperate veneer. Doris, her dream also shattered, leaves her new finery behind; a long shot catches Sönderby watching her go from a dark, first-floor window, imprisoned in his loneliness by the square corner of the house on one side and tall, dark trees on the other.

Back in Stockholm, the film ends with an almost identical scene to that which opened it; the same studio, same characters, and the same positions. Susanne, like Marie in *Summer Interlude*, absorbs the effect of her affair with Henrik; she tears up a letter from him suggesting a meeting on his forthcoming business trip. Doris is reunited with Palle – the experience having made no mark on her – her romantic dream of 'love' apparently intact. Susanne's reaction reflects more grief denied than happiness accepted; she uses her grief as a stage in her approach to maturity. Doris, Susanne and Sönderby can be seen as three stages in the same process, reflecting the fallacy inherent in preferring dream to reality.

Smiles of a Summer Night (1955), the last of this group of three films, marks the beginning of Bergman's international recognition, heralded by the award of a prize for its 'poetic humour' at the Cannes Film Festival. Like *A Lesson in Love*, it is a comedy but with rough patches polished and loose ends tied in; in the same way, the comic surface overlies the tragic undercurrent, the pain of real life, made more distinct by its setting of artificial and elegant formality in turn-of-the-century aristocratic and *haut-bourgeois* life. It is an extremely theatrical film, both in visual effect and in the sense that every happening has been carefully staged. Bergman considers his work for the stage to be as important as his film work, and clearly here he combines his skill in both fields. It has a great deal of the predictability and inevitability of farce about it; Bergman calls it a 'construction' and John Simon likens it to an elegant dance – quadrille or minuet – in which however many changes of partner take place, the dancers always return to their original choice at the end.

Egerman is a successful lawyer, approaching middle age; Anne, his second wife, is only nineteen. He has a son, Henrik, fresh from theological studies and intent on going into the Church. Egerman has in the past been the lover of the actress Desirée Armfeldt; she still loves him, though their affair has long been over; she is now the mistress of Count Carl Magnus Malcolm. He in turn is married to Charlotte, a childhood acquaintance of Anne Egerman. Henrik, repressed and inhibited, is in love with Anne who, it gradually becomes apparent, is also in love with him. Her relationship to Egerman is more that of daughter than wife; he loves her more as an ideal of beauty and innocence than as a woman. Although they have been married for two years, the marriage is unconsummated and Egerman is content to wait for her decision to lose her virginity.

This intricate web of relationships comes to life when Egerman, noticing that Desirée is playing the lead in the current production at the local theatre, buys tickets for himself and Anne. While he and Anne are taking a nap before dinner, he dreams of Desirée, speaking her name out loud. Anne hears it; at the theatre her realization that the actress on stage is called Desirée arouses her suspicion. She begins to weep and Egerman takes her home. Later he visits Desirée in her dressing room; they discuss his relationship with Anne, Desirée expressing surprise at his admitting to loving her, an admission he never made about Desirée herself. Still, she has her emotions under control and will not concede him anything until he makes a move towards her; she is one step ahead of Susanne in *Journey into Autumn*. The most assured and complete character in the film, she is a controlling factor in much of the action, her self-confidence allowing her to manipulate the rest of the cast like a benevolent puppeteer.

At Desirée's house Egerman finds himself in a typically farcical situation. Having fallen into a large puddle and soaked his clothes on the way there, he has been dressed by Desirée in a nightshirt and dressing-gown belonging to her lover Malcolm. A captain of dragoons, Malcolm is supposedly safely engaged on manoeuvres, but he makes his appearance unexpectedly, having got twenty-four hours leave ('Three hours coming here, nine hours for you [Desirée], five hours for my wife, and three hours back') and confronts Egerman, whom he submits to the humiliation of walking home in the borrowed shirt. Egerman, earlier showing himself to be Malcolm's match in an exchange of thinly veiled insults, accepts this with the resignation of a man who knows himself at a disadvantage in matters of physical violence, his dignified acceptance of the inevitable contrasting throughout the film with the caricature of conventional masculinity in Malcolm. Of the two, Malcolm is in fact the more pitiable, like Caligula in *Frenzy* much more the victim of his own psyche than victimizer of Egerman. Malcolm's bombastic egotism is gradually revealed as a frantic façade to the gaping void of his personality.

Desirée contrives to assemble the protagonists for a weekend at her mother's country estate, intending to manipulate the possible permutation of couples so that all end up with the desired partner. She makes a plan with Charlotte to allow her to get Malcolm back, wanting Egerman for herself: 'Men can never see what's good for them. We have to help them find their way'. The plan goes into action at dinner. It is a summer night, the ambiance at the table electric with the tension between the various characters assembled together, and sultry with the erotic tone of the conversation.

Charlotte bets Malcolm that she can seduce Egerman in fifteen minutes. The tension breaks as they drink their wine – 'to every cask filled with this wine a drop of milk from the swelling breast of a woman who has just given birth to her first child and a drop of seed from a young stallion are added' – when Henrik, already upset by the effect of the conversation on his tender susceptibilities, reacts so violently that he breaks his glass and loses his temper with his father. Anne calms Henrik down, whereupon Egerman realizes what the two have not yet admitted to each other that they are in love, and that Anne will never love him as he could wish. Henrik goes off to his room, and the rest of the party disperses, Anne retiring to bed, the others to drink coffee in the Yellow Pavilion.

Henrik tries unsuccessfully to hang himself. The sequence is not unlike the hilarious suicide attempt of Marianne in *A Lesson in Love*. Staggering about the room, he unwittingly sets in motion machinery dating from the time when the house was a royal residence, installed to facilitate the king's assignations; Anne's bed, with her in it, slides through the wall from the adjoining room. The two declare their love and, deliriously joyful, elope in a carriage without further ado. As they leave, Anne throws off her white veil (a symbol of her final rejection of virginity) and Egerman, who, unnoticed, has witnessed the elopement, returns to the pavilion where he meets Charlotte. Malcolm – sent by Desirée, who recognizes a danger to herself in Egerman's present vulnerable state – thinking that the seduction wager is being played out, sends Charlotte away, forcing Egerman to participate in a round of Russian roulette. His remark to Desirée – 'I can tolerate somebody dallying with my mistress, but if anybody touches my wife then I become a tiger' – neatly sums up his character, balancing his earlier and almost identical statement to Charlotte, in which the positions of the words 'mistress' and 'wife' were reversed.

The Russian roulette sequence is a tragicomic exercise in humiliation. Egerman continues in his role as the evening's victim; he is in real fear that the revolver will go off. Unlike Malcolm he has not the advantage of knowing that the weapon is loaded with a soot-filled blank cartridge. The suspense in this scene is very real, since the audience does not know either, a pressure which is deliberately maintained after the shot is heard, since far from witnessing the event all we see is the outside of the pavilion door. The actual identity of the victim is not revealed until Malcolm appears; the shot of Egerman, baffled and blackened, while lacking the impact of Albert's attempt to shoot himself in *Sawdust and Tinsel*, is nonetheless very moving. Desirée cleans Egerman's face. When she asks him if it hurts, his reply 'Yes, it hurts, hurts, hurts' does not refer to any possible pistol wound. He falls asleep and Desirée leaves the pavilion, pocketing the photographs of Anne which are on the sideboard; that episode in Egerman's life is over. The Malcolms are reunited, the Count swearing to be faithful 'in my way', which is to say, not at all.

The film ends on an idyllic note, with everything arranged more or less satisfactorily. Petra, the Egermans' maid, and Frid, old Mrs Armfeldt's groom, have since dinner been engaged in uncomplicatedly happy dalliance – shots of them and their simple courting appear throughout the action of the main plot, forming an *allegro* counterpoint to its *maestoso*. The title of the film comes from Frid, the three smiles of the summer night being respectively for young lovers, for 'the clowns, the fools, the incorrigible' and for 'the grieving, the sleepless ... the frightened, the lonely'.

Elegant, frothy period comedy though it is, *Smiles of a Summer Night* is like a meringue with a hard centre. As in his other comedies, Bergman points to the underlying tragedies of life, while the recurrent motifs of his *œuvre* gain by their juxtaposition with laughter. The film conveniently summarizes his work thus far, marking an emergent international reputation and the real end of apprenticeship to his craft.

CHAPTER THREE

THE CANONICAL FILMS

Critical opinion naturally differs over a choice of Bergman's most important films. This part – aiming at a balanced selection from the sixteen years between *The Seventh Seal* and *Cries and Whispers* – ignores four films, of which only one, *The Virgin Spring (Jungfruk-* *ällen)* (1959), might reasonably lay claim to inclusion in the canon. Although *So Close to Life (Nära livet)* (1957) is interesting as a near documentary study of three women in a maternity ward, and *Now About These Women* (1964), a satirical comedy, is notable as Berg-man's first colour film, they and *The Devil's Eye (Djävulens öga)* (1960) – a highly theatrical piece of trivia – are essentially minor films. *The Virgin Spring* shares with *So Close to Life* a script by Ulla Isaksson; like *The Seventh Seal* too, it has a medieval setting, but it is much more naturalistic in style and less clearly personal than many of Bergman's previous films. Its rather overblown Christian conclusion offers, however, a brief return to spiritual certainty before Bergman, in his trilogy, finally confirms a God-forsaken world.

International Breakthrough

The Seventh Seal

What Peter Cowie called Bergman's 'exercise in tempered expres-sionism' opened up new ground in the art of the film when it was released in 1956. It dealt with a serious subject – the fate of man in a world abandoned by God – and employed in the treatment of that theme a crisp acting style and a stark technical manner. Even now, over twenty years later, the film's visual splendour has not diminished. Its doomsday metaphor is just as meaningful now as it was in the late fifties, when the cold war was only just beginning to thaw and mankind was made aware that in the silos of the super-powers was stored enough nuclear potential to destroy all life on this planet. Today that political shadow is over us once again, in addition to the preoccupation of the last decade with ecological disaster. So Bergman's image of the Knight and his Squire wandering through a plague-stricken Sweden at the time of the Crusades remains a potent one. Like the people in the inn, we are terrified of portents, and wonder how long we have to survive. We may be more sophisticated than medieval man in our technology, but his fear remains our fear: that we do not know what will be the manner of our dying. The film explores this problem under the aegis of the Book of Revelation, from which the title of the film (the seventh seal, which the lamb broke and provoked a silence in Heaven for about half an hour) is taken. The silence of Heaven is shown to be the silence of God himself. The ominous boom and the image of the hovering sea-eagle which opens the film sets the tone for Bergman's exploration of human fear and metaphysical emptiness.

It was his first major movie. He had, of course, achieved an international breakthrough with *Smiles of a Summer Night* the previous year, but though this gay erotic comedy, tinged with sadness, was characteristic of one aspect of his style, it was more truly the culmination of his apprenticeship years than the start of a new era. It was, in fact, *The Seventh Seal* which established Ingmar Bergman in the eyes of most discerning film critics as a major talent in the world of film. Although by no means perfect, it is a film which retains its power and influence nearly a generation later. This is to a large extent because, like *Smiles of a Summer Night*, it is a profoundly compassionate work. The movie offers real people who, despite the exotic costume they wear, appeal to us as likeable or repulsive individuals. The renegade priest Raval is as hateful as Squire Jons is attractive. The juggler's wife Mia is as fresh and innocent as the blacksmith's wife is sordid. The Knight, who might at first seem cold and humourless, is shown in an attractive light by his long-lost wife when she gazes up at him in the closing

sequence in the castle and recognizes in his eyes the boy who went
away so many years before. Earlier, the Knight had described how
happy he had been with his young bride before he set off for his
ten-year service in the Holy Land, and we realize clearly that this
tormented man had once been a carefree bridegroom. His present
anguish makes all the more intolerable the suffering of a world
which inflicts this decline upon him. Little wonder that he says, in
one of the most telling indictments of man's fate made in the course
of the film, 'we make an idol of our fear and call it God'. When the
Knight prays at the altar in the church he looks up at the face of
Christ on the cross, but Jesus's eyes are turned upwards, his mouth
open as if in a cry of anguish (in *Winter Light* there is an equally
tortured crucifix in Tomas' vestry); even the Son of God is
abandoned in this desolate universe. In his debate with the Knight
in the confessional, Death slyly suggests that it may be pointless to
call out to God since there is perhaps no one there. The Knight
replies 'Then life is an outrageous horror. No one can live in the
face of death knowing that all is nothingness' (p. 28); and it is
something he refuses to accept throughout the story. Death taunts
him later on: 'Don't you ever stop asking questions?', to which the
Knight replies: 'No, I'll never stop' (p. 68). Not only is he faced on
the one hand with quizzical Death, he has on the other the sardonic
asperity of his Squire to contend with. When he looks into the eyes
of the young witch to see if she can tell him anything about the
Devil (who, he reasons, is bound to know something about God if
anybody does), Jons presses him to reveal what she sees. The
Knight does not answer his question. Jons returns to the attack:
'Who watches over that child?' he asks. 'Is it the Angels, or God,
or the Devil, or only the emptiness? Emptiness, my lord!' To this
the Knight replies that that cannot be. Jons will not let him get
away with this. 'Look at her eyes, my lord', he insists. 'Her poor
brain has just made a discovery. Emptiness under the moon'
(p. 69). Their argument continues through to the end of the film:
the tormented belief of the Knight is continually being rebutted by
the nihilistic agnosticism of his Squire. At the very end, the two
appear to be addressing God, but are in fact continuing their
argument together:

KNIGHT: From our darkness we call out to Thee,
Lord. Have mercy on us because we are small and
frightened and ignorant.

JONS [*bitterly*]: In the Darkness where You are supposed to be, where all of us probably are . . . in the
darkness You will find no one to listen to Your cries
or be touched by Your sufferings. Wash Your tears
and mirror Yourself in Your indifference.

KNIGHT: God, You who are somewhere, who *must* be
somewhere, have mercy upon us.

JONS: I could have given you a herb to purge you of
your worries about eternity. Now it seems to be too
late. But in any case, feel the immense triumph of
this last minute when you can still roll your eyes and
move your toes.

(p. 81)

The Knight's wife Karin puts a stop to this wrangling with
lulling words: 'Quiet, quiet,' she says. Jons replies: 'I shall be
silent, but under protest.' As so often in Bergman's films, it is the
women who cut through the intellectual posturings and dishonesty
of the men with a simple gesture of denial. But the full affirmation
of the film is reserved for the girl whom Jons has taken on as his
housekeeper. Throughout the film she is silent, possibly mute.
But immediately after Karin has ordered the men to stop their
bickering, the girl moves forward and falls on her knees. Her
words, 'It is finished', are, of course, those used by Christ in similar
circumstances on the cross; they are here, in their way, words of
affirmation. This girl, who has seen much suffering, and even tried
to alleviate it (it is she who wishes to give water to Raval as he dies,
although he had threatened to rape her earlier), is obviously the
appropriate member of the group to welcome death with open
arms. Both Jons and the Knight refuse in their different ways to
bow to the inevitable; it is the women, and in particular this
long-suffering girl, who show that the inevitable can, and indeed
must, be accepted with dignity. It is the only possible answer to
the Knight's fierce assertion that no one can live in the face of death
in the knowledge that all is nothingness: the girl shows that one

can, and indeed that one does. Like Karin who welcomes the weary
travellers to her home, even though she has only just been reunited
with her husband, the girl has forcibly to be restrained from
attempting to help her dying enemy; these positive actions stand
in sharp contrast to the ultimately sterile disputations of their
menfolk. The contrast between male restless aggression and female
passivity and resignation runs deeper than the other contrasts on
which the film is built, between light and dark, between life and
death, youth and old age, between asceticism (on the part of the
Knight) and hedonism (on the part of the Squire), between fanatic-
ism and tolerance, comedy (in the episode between the blacksmith
and the actor) and tragedy (in the stoical reunion between Karin
and her husband), and between the concrete and physical on the
one hand and the abstract and metaphysical on the other. *The
Seventh Seal* can almost be said to live by such contrasts. The robber
of the dead, Raval, is denied water, but the wrongly-convicted
'witch' is succoured by the Knight before she dies. Moreover the
Knight, who otherwise seems capable only of expressing his metaphysical distress in tormented accents, does succeed in carrying out
the one good action he promises Death if given a respite: this
action, of course, is to permit Jof and Mia to escape from the death
which will engulf the whole of their little band. And finally there is
the contrast between the Knight's obsessive rationalism and Jof's
intuitive lyricism.

In an interview with Birgitta Steene, Bergman criticized his old
films for what he called their 'stilted literary language' (*Focus on The
Seventh Seal*, p. 43). It was not until much later, with *The Silence*,
that Bergman decided to make a film in which he used minimal
dialogue. At the stage of his career when he made *The Seventh Seal*
he was still inclined to employ a great deal of dialogue – even if
some of it is rather pretentious. Likewise, as Colin Young points
out (*Focus on The Seventh Seal*, p. 61), the choice of music in *The
Seventh Seal* seems 'oddly theatrical'. But these verbal and musical
awkwardnesses are of no significance compared with the majestic
construction of the movie, in which, as Robert Gessner has shown,
curiosity centres upon the length of the reprieve granted to the
Knight from death, although the outcome of his chess game is

pre-ordained (*Focus on The Seventh Seal*, p. 130). This firm structure gives the film its undoubted dramatic power to shock and move us. Another aspect of its structural authority is the way in which the end reflects and comments upon the beginning: the film opens at dawn, though this new day brings little relief because 'a hot gust of wind blows across the colourless sea' (p. 13); but at the end the sea is described as wafting a strong and fragrant wind of sunrise across to Jof and Mia at the start of a fresh day and a new beginning in their life. The overnight storm has cleared the oppressive heat which hung ominously over the events of the previous day that culminated in the deaths of the Knight's band of followers.

Although the most memorable images are probably those of the burning of the witch or of Karin reading from the Book of Revelation at the last supper in the castle, considerable human warmth pervades the film and emerges triumphant at the end. And despite the odd pretentious note, the dialogue is often witty. The banter between Death and the actor, Skat, who hides in the tree from the wild animals in the forest with the intention of going in search of his companions at first light is a good example. He hears sawing, and assuming that woodcutters are working in the forest even at that late hour, he looks down and notices a figure in black. 'Who are you?' he asks. The cowled figure looks up at him and winks. Skat is terrified when he recognizes Death, who tells him he is sawing down the tree because Skat's time is up. Then follows this piece of dialogue:

> SKAT: It won't do. I haven't got time.
> DEATH: So you haven't got time.
> SKAT: No, I have my performance.
> DEATH: Then it's cancelled because of death.
> SKAT: My contract.
> DEATH: Your contract is terminated.
> SKAT: My children, my family.
> DEATH: Shame on you, Skat!   (p. 74)

Skat admits that he is guilty of a lie, but this does not mollify Death, who continues sawing at the tree. Skat asks if there is any way of getting off, whether there aren't any special rules for actors.

Death says there are none in this case. Skat asks whether there are
any loopholes or exceptions, and even whether Death will accept a
bribe. Death gives no reply to all of this but continues to saw;
finally, with Skat shouting 'Help! Help!', the tree falls, and a little
squirrel then jumps on to the stump and nibbles away briskly at the
crumbs of sawdust. The light-hearted treatment of Skat's death is
intended to contrast strongly with the gruesome end of Raval soon
afterwards, and is characteristic of the way in which the film plays
upon different moods, alternating between levity and solemnity;
this accounts in large measure for its charm and psychological
plausibility.

Wild Strawberries

> *Film as an art form ... should*
> *communicate psychic states, not*
> *merely project pictures of external*
> *action* (Bergman)

Bergman shares with few other contemporary directors the ability
to maintain a high degree of precision in his observations of
physical and psychical phenomena. Rarely careless or insipid in
approach, the technical construction of his early pieces is nonetheless uneven. It is in *Wild Strawberries*, arguably his most formally
exquisite work, that Bergman first achieved that outstandingly
rigorous balance of emotional force, psychological depth and structural finesse peculiar to most of his later films.

The basic theme of *Wild Strawberries* is an individual's journey
into self-knowledge through confrontation with the past. In dealing with a need for personal redefinition and redirection, it recalls
Summer Interlude, Sawdust and Tinsel, and its immediate predecessor
The Seventh Seal. The problems in *Wild Strawberries* are as great as in
The Seventh Seal but more personal and psychological; the question
of God's presence or absence, so crucial to the denouement of *The
Seventh Seal*, gives way to a vaguer notion of order, that personal
salvation and peace of mind depend on simple manifestations of

human love and understanding rather than on divine or super-natural intervention. As in *The Seventh Seal*, where mutual love and devotion save Jof and Mia from the clutches of Death, so in *Wild Strawberries* Isak Borg can only resolve his dilemma by his own efforts to love those around him and to acknowledge his weaknesses and past failures.

Bergman uses the large Swedish wild strawberry (*smultron*) to symbolize peace and happiness in *Summer Interlude*, where Marie and Henrik pick the fruit together, and in *The Seventh Seal*, where Jof and Mia offer milk and strawberries to the Knight at dusk. The association is traditional in Sweden – in Strindberg's *A Dream Play*, for instance, the Officer recalls 'wild strawberries and milk for supper' at the age of seven. The symbol also has a darker side – in ripening only once, briefly, before disappearing, the berry represents the fleeting nature of both beauty and happiness. As the title suggests, this ambiguous image characterizes the fluctuating mood of *Wild Strawberries*. This rhythmic movement derives from the ageing Professor Borg's journey by car from Stockholm to Lund, the university city in southern Sweden where he is to receive an honorary doctorate. Successive dreams and encounters on the way force Borg to realize his egotism, intolerance and emotional sterility. His overriding fault is an unwillingness to face these facts. Though the film has a complex structure, Borg passes relatively simply from a state of complacency through despair to provisional peace of mind. Feelings of guilt and humiliation under-line the painful transition, obliging Borg to alter his selfish out-look in order to expiate the past and survive. This Strindbergian pattern of mortification and atonement explains why *Wild Straw-berries* has much in common with *A Dream Play*, in which the Poet remarks 'surely suffering is redemption and death deliverance,' while the Daughter of Indra says 'Life is hard. But love conquers everything.' Bergman acknowledges the influence on *Wild Straw-berries* of this play and *To Damascus*, along with the work of the nineteenth-century Swedish author C.J.L. Almqvist. In theme and plot, as Birgitta Steene points out, *Wild Strawberries* may owe something to Sjöström's *The Phantom Carriage* (1921), a possibility reinforced by the image of a horse-drawn hearse in Borg's first dream. The immediate inspiration of the film, however, was a journey made by Bergman from Stockholm to the province of Dalarna, during which he stopped at Uppsala and, reliving childhood memories, decided to make a film exploring the past from the vantage point of the present: 'someone coming along, perfectly realistically, and suddenly opening a door and walking into his childhood. And then walking round the corner of the street and coming into some other period of his life, and everything still alive and going on as before' (*Bergman on Bergman*, p. 133).

The film takes the form of an alternation between events on the journey and various dreams. The sophistication of the dream sequences recalls *Prison*, while the blend of reality and fantasy again points to Strindberg whose remarks, in the 'Author's Note' to *A Dream Play*, could easily apply to Borg's experience:

> The characters split, double, redouble, evaporate, condense, scatter, and converge. But one consciousness remains above all of them: the dreamer's . . . Sleep, the liberator, appears often as painful, but, when the torture is at its peak, waking comes reconciling suffering with reality.

The subtle counterpoint of time, place, image and character gives the film a musical structure but, as Robin Wood points out, 'the impression given is not of self-conscious and grandiose pretensions but of an artist expressing his natural affinities' (p. 73). The main theme sustains daring yet controlled variations, the solo parts are dynamic and clear, the whole a complete orchestration of Borg's day of reckoning.

The journey, then, is both a literal and a metaphorical basis of the film, as is true also of *Sawdust and Tinsel, Journey into Autumn, The Seventh Seal, The Virgin Spring* and *The Silence*. Other Bergman films include a journey as part of the action; such sequences often contain critical developments, like Tomas' drive from Mittsunda to Frostnäs churches in *Winter Light*, with two significant stops on the way. Furthermore, as in that film, Bergman echoes the mood of *Wild Strawberries* in his depiction of the weather, which undergoes almost as many changes as Borg's disposition itself. This atmospheric support permeates both waking and dreaming time. Bergman's 1970 production of *A Dream Play*, for the Royal Dramatic Theatre of Stockholm, began with the Poet brooding at his desk; *Diary of a Country Priest*, a film by Bresson — whom Bergman admires — begins with the hero writing his diary. Appropriately, then, Bergman opens *Wild Strawberries* with an introductory monologue by Borg, as he writes in a diary, telling us of his wilful solitude, pedantry and testiness. His defensive isolation anticipates later films like *Shame* and *A Passion*, where it becomes a basic theme. Bergman admits that he had himself in mind at the time. The opening sequence testifies already to Bergman's compositional skill, as for instance in the close-up of a chess set, recalling the contest in *The Seventh Seal* between Death and the Knight, here suggesting Borg's pawn-like treatment of others. Framed pictures of relatives are noticeably visible in the same shot where we can make out his son Evald. Close-up or middle close-up shots of other pictures follow; his mother, his daughter-in-law Marianne, his deceased wife Karin. Thus, from the outset, Bergman establishes firmly the ironic link between generations that plays such an important part in Borg's situation. The monologue also includes Borg's assertion that he tries to keep abreast of bacteriological research, an additional irony in view of his ignominious professional display in a subsequent dream.

Like the protracted flashback in *Sawdust and Tinsel*, the first dream sequence — based on a recurrent Bergman dream — occurs soon after the film begins. Images of disintegration and fracture dominate this nightmare: looking up at an optician's sign Borg sees a pair of eyes, one of which seems gouged, beneath a handless clock face; he approaches a motionless insubstantial figure only to observe it fall to the ground and split open, oozing 'blood'; the wheel of a passing hearse breaks loose and rolls toward him in a series of terrifying low-angle shots. The strange location — an empty, uninviting city street in harsh sunlight — is uncannily silent apart from grinding axles (as the hearse sways against a street lamp) and distant tolling bells, a sound repeated in the chilling urban shots at the beginning of *Persona*. This enigmatic setting is further comparable to the city of Timoka in *The Silence*, where

Bergman again relates bright sunlight to fear, an association to which he frequently refers, as in *Bergman on Bergman* (p. 78): 'My nightmares are always saturated in sunshine ... It's like a threat, something ... terrifying ... When I see a cloudless sky I feel the world's coming to an end.' Although dazzled by the sunlight, Borg is cold, confirming the physical as well as psychical illogicalities of the dream. The handless timepieces coincide with Borg's thumping heart, a synchronization of sound and image track repeated during the visit to his mother when he experiences a similar shock. Bergman further emphasises Borg's terror by means of tracking shots as the professor tries to escape from the claustrophobic scene but succeeds only in encountering the human dummy, with its light mask-like face against a dark background suggesting a grotesque reflection of Borg's distraction. The shot typifies Bergman's striking black and white contrasts, prominent throughout his work. Furthermore, he uses reverse shots to put the spectator, so to speak, in Borg's shoes as he confronts his image in the coffin that falls from the hearse. Bergman cuts from a low-angle middle long shot of Borg beyond the coffin to a high-angle middle close-up from behind him. As Borg closes in on his 'corpse', which reaches out to pull him into the coffin, Bergman rapidly alternates close-ups of the two face, underlining Borg's panic, until the images virtually merge as the sequence ends with a zoom-in – zoom shots are always used sparingly, though this film contains four – which then cuts to a close-up of Borg asleep in bed. Dream suddenly gives way to reality as Borg wakes fearfully and consoles himself, a familiar experience for Bergman as he says in an interview with A. Alvarez (*The Observer*, 25 January 1976): 'You wake up ... with demons at your breast and hell all around ... I like waking up at four in the morning scared to death.'

After a domestic scene, establishing the relationship between Borg, his daughter-in-law Marianne and his housekeeper Agda, the film introduces the journey by means of two successive dissolves, one to a shot of Borg's car leaving the deserted centre of Stockholm ('borg' means 'city' in Swedish, perhaps a symbolic reference to the professor's emotional emptiness), the other to a shot of the car on a country road. This concise montage allows for coherent yet economical narrative. Bergman consistently defines landscape by brief long shots, like those of Lake Vättern at lunchtime and in the afternoon, which serve also to specify the time of day (the lake is roughly midway between Stockholm and Lund). The shot of an idyllic shoreline as Borg and Marianne approach the summer house of the professor's youth prefigures the final sequence; this charming lake setting, reminiscent in mood of *Summer with Monika* and *Summer Interlude* on the Stockholm archipelago, may owe something to a scene on a similarly wooded coastline with boats and flags in *A Dream Play*. These shots, often involving a tilt up or down of the camera to reveal scenery, show how Bergman interweaves his images without the conscious realization of the spectator. Thus we see the car, then the lake; or the lake, then the lunch table.

Arriving at the summer house, Borg rediscovers the wild strawberry patch which gives the film its Swedish title, unloosing in Proustian fashion vivid memories of his boyhood. With an intuition that this was to be 'a day of decision,' his mind wanders and he falls asleep, precipitating the film's first flashback and second dream sequence. It is a pleasant dream, portraying Borg as he really is, looking in on his youth. A dissolve into a middle long shot changes the house to its former state. As in the second flashback, piano music accompanies the sequence. Borg meets his first love, his cousin Sara. The imagery is prefigurative: we see his cousin Sigbritt's baby sleeping in a cradle under a calm sky, an image revisualized unpleasantly in the third dream; Borg enters the corridor of the house, later to become a gloomy passage to his examination room. Standing in the dark hallway, he observes the family breakfasting in the bright, airy dining room. This scene, like the subsequent lunch, consists largely of middle shots, as if Bergman here seeks to place in perspective the various individuals flooding Borg's memory. The sustained contrast between light and dark is crystallized in the image of a glass door, which is not only Bergman's own memory of a door in the house in Uppsala's Slottsgatan (an association rekindled colourfully in Winkelman's house in *A Passion*) but also peculiarly reminiscent of a larder door remembered from the age of four by the Officer in *A Dream Play*.

The dream ends as Borg suddenly notices the presence of another Sara, a young hitch-hiker who, with her boyfriends Anders and Viktor, joins Borg and Marianne on their journey. This Sara indulges in lighthearted banter with Borg, provoking him to refer to his lost love as 'a now rather beautiful little old lady', ironically stressing the onward march of time. Indeed, the whole journey gradually reveals Borg's mistakes and regrets. In appearance, young Sara reminds him painfully of her namesake, while his behaviour towards Marianne — like towards Agda at the outset — reveals his egotism, intolerance and insensitivity to others. A series of reverse middle close-ups of the two companions establishes their mutual antithesis. At one point, he indicates disapproval of her cigarette smoking yet defends male cigar smoking. Marianne complains that she knows him only as a father-in-law and Borg admits that he relates impersonally to Marianne, though she puts the words into his mouth:

> ISAK: Now, if I am honest, I must say that I've enjoyed having you around the house.
> MARIANNE: Like a cat.
> ISAK: Like a cat, or a human being, it's the same thing.
> (*Four Screenplays*, p. 180)

The matter of the loan to Evald unveils another facet of Borg's hardheartedness as well as, like the smoking incident, prefiguring a turning point in the film.

The confrontation in the second dream between Borg and his cousin shows her awareness of one of his chief weaknesses — the split between his intellect and emotions, a theme on which Bergman dwells repeatedly in his anxiety about the relationship of the artist/intellectual to the 'world of men.' Sara emphasizes this during the third dream sequence, when it really affects Borg, whereas he treats earlier criticism with smug seniority. 'Extremely intellectual' and 'morally aloof' to his cousin, he initially impresses but later alienates her. Such qualities become defects: cerebral detachment sours into solipsistic coldness; Isak turns icy.

The journey continues until a car crash pitches Borg and companions in with Berit and Sten Alman. This brief but painful involvement dramatizes an idea which underlies, for instance, *Winter Light* and *Shame*: that however much one tries, one cannot avoid the responsibility of coping with other people's intrusion into one's life. The Almans squabble relentlessly (they are caricatures of a Swedish critic and his wife, for whom Bergman had little respect) and, Borg later tells Marianne, their bitter exchanges remind him of his own unhappy marriage. The couple's mutual humiliation is a foretaste of Borg's own shame, while their cynicism reflects his gentler but equally ruthless attitude and contrasts sharply with the naive idealism of Anders and Viktor, whose intellectual disagreement also leads to blows. Indeed, it is because of their influence on the 'children' that Marianne ejects the Almans from the car. Berit's last words – 'forgive us if you can' – also foreshadow Borg's eventual repentance.

The Almans' theatrical behaviour, suggestive both of *The Face* and *Persona*, supports the revelation – mocked by Sten – that Berit is an ex-actress; he refers to the contrived spontaneity of a film 'take', an example of Bergman's aesthetic reflexiveness evident also in *Prison*, *Persona* and *A Passion*. The car accident further resembles *A Passion*, in which Anna Fromm – crippled from a previous crash – and Andreas Winkelman have a narrow escape as their car swerves off the road. Even the shot in *Wild Strawberries*, of 'road ahead seen through the car windscreen. Track forwards with the car ...', is virtually identical to the composition of crash shots in *A Passion*. At the moment of danger, Bergman intensifies the sense of shock by a rapid succession of shots from opposing angles, placing the viewer in the driving seat. Then as they all leave the scene of the mishap in one car, Bergman shows his compositional skill in a front shot of all six passengers with Alman, Berit and Marianne in middle close-up, creating a fine study in facial expression.

After the Almans leave in disgrace, there is some light relief in a filling station scene with Max von Sydow relegated from Knight (*The Seventh Seal*) to pump attendant. Yet the sequence is not totally without serious purpose; Åkerman (von Sydow) and his wife embarrassingly but effectively make Borg realize his former worth as a country doctor before intellectual careerism deprived the locality of his services. Similarly, Borg can later realize the irony of young Sara's flattering speech in which she lauds him for every attribute that he must surely now regret.

The lunch scene, though anticipating Borg's nightmarish examination in his failure to remember a poem, is in general a relaxed sequence preceding the drastic change in mood when he visits his mother. It also permits Bergman, through Anders and Viktor, to dwell on the conflict between scientific rationalism and religious faith that haunts so much of his work. Moreover, that Anders intends to be a priest and Viktor a doctor likens the debate to the 'fight' between Theology and Medicine in *A Dream Play*.

The uneasy scene at the house of Borg's mother reveals another structural base: the chain of five generations from his grandmother to Marianne's unborn child. We sense a congenital coldness transmitted from the deathly old woman through Borg to its extreme in Evald, who plainly expresses both a wish to die and a refusal of procreative responsibility. This unwilling inheritance is ironically underscored by his grandmother's remark: 'Ten children, and all of them dead except Isak.' An old portrait on the wall behind Borg's mother appears to depict these several generations of the family, and suggests her anachronistic existence, amidst inanimate reminders of the past like dolls and toy soldiers, which she unearths for Borg and Marianne to see. This brings to mind *A Dream Play* in which the officer Alfred and the Daughter of Indra have to face an invalid mother. Borg's mother, dressed in black, complains of coldness, reiterating her son's sensation in the first dream. In this sequence, as in *Persona*, Bergman pays special attention to hands, culminating in the old woman's presentation of a handless watch to Borg, setting off once more the thudding heartbeat of the first dream. This incident plays on Borg's unconscious fears: the light fades appropriately, weather turns bad. By the time they leave, Borg is already drawn closer to the life that is in Marianne who, by deciding to have her child, represents escape from this congenital frigidity. The whole film, in fact, contrasts old and new ways of life, for though in retrospect the young travellers are, as Bergman admits, corny and dated stereotypes, their presence helps Bergman lay the foundations of his personal probe into changing social values, perfected in the island dramas, and in *The Touch, Cries and Whispers* and *Scenes from a Marriage*.

The third dream sequence – a second flashback to Borg's youth – represents the nadir of his fortune. Everything has pointed ominously to a crisis; a low angle shot of screeching birds, then a shot of lake and sky with the sound of distant thunder dissolves to the basket of wild strawberries spilled on the grass. What was glorious summer is now stormy discontent; cousin Sara, strangely distant and stern, holds up a mirror to Borg, forcing him to reflect on his ageing narcissism. In this dream, Borg tries to ignore his own reflected gaze but Sara insists that he 'can't bear the truth,' a sequence of reverse shots emphasizing their mutual alienation. Sara then joins Sigfrid inside the summer house; Borg, trying to attract their attention from outside, catches his hand on a nail. This symbolic notion of martyrdom relates not only to *Sawdust and Tinsel, The Seventh Seal* – in which a girl burns at the stake and processional flagellants bear crosses – and *A Passion* but also *Persona*, during which we twice see a nail being driven through the palm of a hand.

The illogicality of dream takes over completely as the interior of the house becomes an examination room where Alman subjects a terrified Borg to tests of his professional competence, accusing him of various offences. The use of soft focus and a middle close-up of Borg shakingly pouring water into a glass demonstrates his panic, intensified by incomprehensible words on a blackboard, language as alien as that of the Timokans in *The Silence*. Alman (all-man) pronounces Borg guilty and sentences him to loneliness as, in *A Dream Play*, the Officer is sent back to school to endure the same lessons until he matures. For Borg, worse is still to come: Alman then leads him through a reptilian swamp to witness his wife's adultery in a forest clearing. Light-dark contrasts again heighten this eerie scene. Only by facing up to his wife's remarks can Borg understand that the reason for his broken marriage was his condescending, self-righteous forgiveness of her act.

As this nightmare ends, Bergman contrasts its gruesome imagery with a shot of the young travellers picking flowers, so returning to a scene where the storm has passed, both in actuality and symbolically. Thoroughly drained and humiliated, Borg must now change his outlook or suffer emotional death. Yet he must face one more obstacle in the way of his regeneration: initial responsibility for Evald's selfishness. This is the subject of a flashback in which Marianne relates a showdown between herself and Evald (in their car) one rainy afternoon. Evald opposes bringing a child into what he considers an absurd, painful world:

> MARIANNE: That is only an excuse.
> EVALD: Call it whatever you want. Personally I was an unwelcome child in a marriage which was a nice imitation of hell . . . Indifference, fear, infidelity and guilt feelings — these were my nurses.
>
> *(Four Screenplays*, p. 226)

In order to show their interrelationship, Bergman cuts repeatedly from close-up of Marianne to middle close-up of Evald, always with her voice over; later, in a similar way, Bergman replaces Evald's image with that of Borg, stressing their common identity. Drives in the rain often accompany such conflicts in Bergman's films, as in Alma's discovery (through an unsealed letter) of Elisabet's patronizing, critical attitude towards her in *Persona*, or the separation of Anna and Andreas after the near crash in *A Passion*.

Arriving at last in Lund, hints of reconciliation underlie the family reunion. Borg has already invited Marianne to smoke and offered to help her to keep both child and husband, small but crucial gestures in his battle for peace of mind. He goes through a ceremony very similar to the doctoral graduation in *A Dream Play*, even to the point of a gun salute (a shot also highly reminiscent of the cannon fire in the *Sawdust and Tinsel* flashback). Bergman here favours low-angle shots to suggest the hierarchical grandeur of academic ritual, following it with a contrasting close-up of Agda giving Borg sleeping pills, thus both returning the action to the domestic plane and bringing out a sense of unreality in the 'refined torture' of the ceremony. It is an apt comment on Borg's belated change of heart that the crowning glory of his career seems boring and pretentious; he appears to be more concerned with apologizing to Agda and releasing Evald from financial obligation, though ironically the latter gesture is misinterpreted. At night, the young travellers serenade Borg beneath his window in a rather sentimental scene that does, however, contain young Sara's declaration of love for Borg, intended as an adolescent effusion but in fact preparing him for a mental reconciliation with his beloved cousin.

This reconciliation occurs in the final dream sequence (the third flashback to bygone days) and prompts one of the most moving codas in cinema. Bergman dissolves to a long shot of the summer house; everything is idyllic again. Sara leads Borg — as his real self — to see his parents sitting by the shore in a serene, painterly scene of intense nostalgia, accompanied by wistful chords on a guitar. Borg, like Frost in *Sawdust and Tinsel*, shouts inaudibly to them but, unlike the tormented clown, his is a contented expression. At this moment, as in his earlier offer to Marianne, Borg recovers the joy of giving and receiving parental love, hitherto repressed by the inbred father complex. He replaces fear and contempt of his parents with a vision of eternal familial communion. The film ends on a note of optimism, revival and relief.

From aesthetic and intellectual standpoints, *Wild Strawberries* is one of Bergman's most satisfying films. Contrasts and parallels fit together like parts of a jigsaw puzzle. Its structural poise creates a total harmony, like a baroque concerto, while Borg's tacit achievement of peace of happiness is unapparent in such complete form in any subsequent Bergman work. In spite of Jof and Mia, *The Seventh Seal* ends with death and storm still in sight: in *Wild Strawberries* the clouds, even if fleetingly, have disappeared without a trace. The conditional resolution of this film gives way to growing doubt and despair, coming to a head in the agnostic fear and arid solitudes of the trilogy. With the possible exception of *The Virgin Spring*, no subsequent work offers as much cause for hope as *Wild Strawberries*, yet even *The Virgin Spring* ends in a forced, sentimental way. *Wild Strawberries* may be too finely honed to bear the emotional force it releases, but for all that it remains an elegant and powerful expression of personal drama.

Three Portraits of the Artist

Sawdust and Tinsel

> *What is good for you is not*
> *always tasty*
> (Granny, in *The Face*)

Sawdust and Tinsel demonstrates clearly that although Bergman bases his cinematic style on certain recurrent ideas and techniques, these elements are freshly effective in each work, a freshness stemming from consistently original material and an imaginative approach. This film presents humiliation, suffering and regeneration as themes; it has a twenty-four hour time span involving a journey. A pallid imitation of *Wild Strawberries* comes to mind, yet *Sawdust and Tinsel* precedes it by four years, emerging distinctively but to lukewarm reception in 1953, between the changing fortune of *Summer with Monika* and the playfulness of *A Lesson in Love*. In fact, *Sawdust and Tinsel* is a very different type of film from *Wild Strawberries*; for all its excursions into dream and psychodrama, the later film is primarily an exercise in naturalistic cinema, built around a highly specific landscape and chronology. Although *Sawdust and Tinsel* reveals small towns, circus plots and countryside, we feel that for the most part these locations might be anywhere along the troupe's arduous route. Moreover, these settings are seen invariably through strained eyes: the circus as grotesque reflection of its own illusions, the town as either unnervingly quiet or embarrassingly crowded, the open road as strewn with images of degradation, dishonour and discomfort.

Sawdust and Tinsel is relatively inexact regarding place and it jumps back and forth in time by means of parallel or truncated sequences. Influenced by Ewald Dupont's *Variety* (Germany, 1925), it is a visual mélange of naturalism and expressionism, occasionally flamboyant in a manner worthy of Bergman's most decorative work: its immediate successor, *A Lesson in Love*, then *Smiles of a Summer Night* and, more recently, *The Silence* and *Hour of the Wolf* – both broaching individual despair in a Godless world yet visually exotic quite unlike others of their theme and vintage. The expressionistic series proper culminates in *The Seventh Seal*, whereafter Bergman develops close-knit 'chamber' works via *So Close to Life* and the trilogy. The visual heterogeneity of *Sawdust and Tinsel* may further be explained by Bergman's use of four photographers, including Hilding Bladh and Sven Nykvist. Bergman himself makes perhaps the most pertinent comparison, responding to an interviewer's suggestion of a stylistic pot pourri in the film by referring to Stravinsky drawing on diverse idioms yet stamping his compositions with a unique musical vision.

Accompanying the credits and establishing an ambiguous mood is music which turns from cheerful fanfare to strident discord. As if in echo of this uneasy suggestion, we see two characteristic stills: one an idealized image of the circus, the other of its irksome life. Mindful of these contrasts, we witness circus wagons crossing a dawn skyline, a chiaroscuro anticipation of the stark silhouettes at the end of *The Seventh Seal*. The shot conveys a feeling of cold, dull weather, stressing the· hardship facing the down-at-the-heels troupe. The sense of reality versus illusion and of impending conflict is reinforced by a series of apparently random shots: the moving caravan is 'overturned' by reflection in some wayside water; in turn we see a horse, wheel, windmill (a natural association with Cervantes) and bear – articulations of the link between continuous movement and animalistic drudgery beneath a glamorous façade. Throughout the film, wind and rain suggest a contagious messiness symbolizing the sordidness of interpersonal relationships; at one point, foul weather hampers the erection of the big top and a rip appears in the canvas. On the driving seat is Jens, clown and coachman (again, the double life), with the circus master Albert Johansson. Jens tells of the time the clown Frost was humiliated by his wife Alma bathing naked for money, the spectacle paid for by a military regiment lounging on the beach.

After this reminiscence the film traces present misfortunes, primarily the conflict between Albert and his equestrian mistress Anne, with Frost and Alma as secondary figures but painful reminders of personal strife. Anne accompanies Albert on a cos-

tume scrounging visit to a municipal theatre, whose affected director Sjöberg patronizes them and mocks Albert openly. Frans, a young leading actor, makes advances to Anne, who deceives herself into thinking that a liaison with him will improve her lot. While Albert is visiting his ex-wife Agda, Anne returns to the theatre, only to be seduced and then rejected by Frans. Meanwhile, Agda equally rejects Albert's return and the disgruntled couple face each other on returning to their dark, claustrophobic caravan. Then Albert and Frost get desperately drunk, finally spilling exuberantly out of the caravan to cavort about the site in bright sunlight.

At the first show that evening, to which the theatre company has been invited in return for the costume loan, Frans taunts Anne, prompting a challenge from Albert who engages the actor in a bloody fistfight, which Frans unfairly but indisputably wins. Anne then comes to Albert's rescue but the show still breaks up in confusion with the circus master staggering off to commit suicide. Unable to pull the trigger on himself, he instead shoots first his mirror image then, much to Alma's chagrin, the sickly old bear. Relieved of tension Albert succumbs to tears, aware that he must now face up to and continue his restless, impecunious but fitting life on the road. In this harsh but honest light, Anne and Albert face a new dawn and the Cirkus Alberti rolls on.

The flashback occurs shortly after the film begins, like Isak Borg's first and similarly harrowing dream in *Wild Strawberries*. For Bergman, this sequence introduces the plot of *Sawdust and Tinsel* as a series of variations on a basic theme of sexual antagonism, thus reversing *Variety*, which evokes the present in a short initial sequence while an extended flashback comprises the rest of the action. According to Jens, the episode occurred seven years previously when Frost worked with Weger's circus.

Cinematically the sequence is notable, chiefly on account of the peculiar image created by Hilding Bladh (from whom Sven Nykvist learned a great deal). Bladh gained his effect by making a negative of the first print, then printing that negative, eliminating the graininess to obtain a pristine black and white image. This searing tone lends a nightmarish quality to the whole sequence, aptly reflecting Frost's and Alma's exposure. This is reinforced by the soundtrack which, by alternating sound with terrifying silence, produces what John Simon calls an 'aural dépaysement' of considerable force. What sound there is consists of cacophonous music, narratival voice-over and natural sound that is limited to the soldiers' laughter – thus rendered all the more derisive – and the faint roar of the sea as Frost strips off. We see Frost shout at the top of his voice but as in dreams nothing is audible – 'the soundless shriek behind the bared teeth', as Bergman says parenthetically in the script of *Winter Light*. Here, as in the speechless opening sequence, is evidence of Bergman's semi-conscious debt to silent cinema, just as the rapid montage recalls Eisenstein in its pace, symbolism and military imagery, although Bergman insists that any similarity is accidental.

Whatever his influences, Bergman repeatedly deploys sound and silence with skill, as in the opening sequences of *The Seventh Seal* and *Winter Light* or in the stunning climax of *Shame*, where silence reigns but for the sparse sound of creaking oars and lapping water. Incidentally, another striking Swedish example of this technique is the opening sequence of Jan Troell's *Interlude in the Marshland* where, in lieu of dialogue, meaning is clearly articulated by shot composition and gesture. This ability to exploit silence may owe something to Swedish taciturnity, something to the natural yet strange quietness that dominates so much of rural Scandinavia to this day.

Frantically attempting to hide their shame, Frost carries Alma back to the circus, stumbling over rocky terrain with the difficulty of movement which occurs in dreams. Frost's intolerable uphill struggle towards sanctuary, out of earshot of the jeering regiment, is his calvary, Alma his cross. Indeed, this symbolic implication is reiterated in a shot of men carrying tent poles which resemble crucifixes and, in the background, by the sound of a crowing cock.

The portrayal of Frost by Anders Ek contributes much both to this sequence and to the film as a whole. Gangling, awkward and angular in feature with a rubber mouth, Ek's expressive agility forcefully depicts this ridiculous clown, a fool's face sewn on his costume over his genitals. In the flashback, in the tense exchange with Albert inside the wagon, his pasty face resembles a mask or death's head, a mien as unnatural as Albert Vogler's in *The Face*, Johan Borg's at the end of *Hour of the Wolf*, or Elisabet Vogler's, when made up to play Electra, in *Persona*.

Ek has used his facial flexibility to good effect in his three other Bergman films to date – as a severe plague-fearing monk in *The Seventh Seal*, a defensive artiste in *The Rite (Riten)* and a weak, depressing Lutheran priest in *Cries and Whispers*, where his self-pitying, nervous utterance on Agnes's death recalls Albert's exclamation, 'Poor all of us, all men who live on earth, and who are, all of us, so scared . . .' Frost eventually dreams that he first shrinks to seed, then disappears totally into Alma, thus expressing his willing submission to woman's greater emotional resilience and connecting him with Bergman's pathetic protagonists of later films – Borg in *Hour of the Wolf*, Rosenberg in *Shame*, Winkelman in *A Passion*, Johan in *Scenes from a Marriage*. Yet, as in these characters, there is the suggestion of both Frost's former strengths or talents since dissipated and his potential for reassertion; for he does command some respect for his loyalty to Alma in the flashback scene and later he emerges as spokesman for the discontented artistes. Even Albert, for the most part spiteful and jealous, ultimately recovers respect for Anne as well as himself.

Indeed, in this 'portrait of the artist', Bergman concentrates on the contradictions inherent in Albert's career. He is at once unsure of his artistic integrity yet sufficiently convinced of it not to abandon his efforts. An entertainer whose life is unentertaining, he rails at being, in his own words, 'stuck in hell', comparing his wretched impoverishment (in the European artistic tradition) with the affluence of his American counterparts. Here Bergman points not only to the emigratory impulse of the time (a theme adopted by Troell in his epic films *The Emigrants* and *The Newcomers*) but also to the diehard ostracism of the artist, irrespective of circus, theatre or cinema background: 'Ten years ago an actor couldn't get a decent room at the town hotel in Jönkoping' (*Bergman on Bergman*, p. 83). Albert knows this only too well; Sjüberg's superior attitude intensifies his humiliation and resentment of his profession. To a great extent Albert's natural extroversion causes problems which the façade of his metier serves to aggravate. Even the name Cirkus Alberti is sham sophistication. Albert is torn between the showman's conceit and underlying self-hatred, a dilemma corroborated by conflict between his innate restlessness and a deep desire for security.

These tensions emerge vividly in the scene where Albert calls on Agda. She exudes calmness and self-sufficiency, an atmosphere captured perfectly by Bergman's set. She keeps a tobacconist's shop in a quiet street and sits sewing in her clean, tidy parlour, surrounded by the contemporary trappings of domestic respectability: pretty tablecloth, flowers in vases, lace curtains, pictures on the wall and ornamental clocks which chime to the absolute regularity of her life. Albert dismisses this as 'emptiness', though he is every bit as shallow; his fancy dress fronts an ordinary shirt in need of repair. Conscious that his rootless, gregarious life has caused their estrangement, he purports nonetheless to scorn Agda's choice, whereas in fact he envies her. Mildly critical of the circus as a 'world of flight, insecurity', she responds to Albert's defensiveness by stating that for her 'it's a quiet street . . . it's fulfilment', a remark which contrasts sharply with Albert's total lack of fulfilment, both in his relationship with her and his own career.

As in his dealings with theatre and townspeople (the police deflate his 'magnificent' parade by confiscating the horses), Albert is humiliated in front of Agda, departing from her in his own words, 'a beggar'. And although the theatrical company share his professional falsity, they too degrade Albert in their pretentiousness and assumed superiority in the artistic hierarchy. Recapitulating the animalistic theme, Sjüberg calls the circus folk 'rabble', 'a pack'; yet he admits, in a witty guise, that their respective careers differ only in that life is at stake in the circus but merely vanity in the theatre. In protraying Sjüberg and Frans as smug narcissists, Bergman exposes the artistic hierarchy as nothing more than shrewd role-playing in which, although some take it more seriously, everyone is ridiculous.

Sexual perversity and exploitation play a major part in the suffering of the characters. This notion recalls particularly *Prison* and is a forerunner of *The Silence*, though it pervades all of Bergman's work. The Albert-Anne-Frans triangle produces taunts, jealousies and vicious games. Frans bribes Anne into submission with an amulet which proves worthless. This vindictiveness explodes, by way of innuendo, in the circus performance with Frans' mockery of Anne. The clowns' knockabout act symbolizes the real beatings; the deformity of the dwarfs reflects the sexual aberrations of the central characters, a motif reiterated more integrally by Bergman in *The Silence*. Likewise, the striking use of harsh sunlight in *The Silence* is anticipated in *Sawdust and Tinsel*, not only in the flashback but also when Albert spies Anne leaving the pawnbroker's after intercourse with Frans. In accordance with Bergman's identification of bright light with anxiety Albert sweats, panics and grimaces. Silhouetted like the cloaked Vogler in *The Face*, he enters the dark caravan menacingly to confront Anne, who literally and figuratively lays her cards on the table, inviting Albert to follow suit. Bergman also stresses the contrast between Anne and Agda by dissolving from the latter's placid expression to an agitated close-up of the former, aroused naively by Frans' melodramatic 'suicide' in rehearsal. Such facial interaction recurs more drastically in *Persona* with a merger of two expressions within a single shot.

The ritualized fight between Albert and Frans turns into savage blood sport, again distinguishing Frans as the clever dilettante who dances his way out of danger. Albert, on the contrary, strikes out wildly like an enraged beast. After this final humiliation, Albert vents his frustration by shooting images of himself: his face in the mirror and the ailing bear. Realization of his cowardice and irresponsibility ironically gives him fresh purpose; weeping alone in the stable, he sees that the 'show must go on' and that the toil, smell and mess of circus life is the only meaningful reality for him.

So the end of *Sawdust and Tinsel*, like *Wild Strawberries*, gives rise to qualified optimism. All is not lost. Faithful translation of the title — 'The Clown's Evening' — implies the critical night and the subsequent dawn. Frans and Albert, the artistes with grand illusions, are the stars of the show, the real clowns. Albert has to publicly endure his own foolishness, like Frost, in order to survive as an individual and make a fresh start. Though Bergman allows his characters this regenerative potential, he articulates the agonies they must endure before making amends. In later films there is simply no escape route; *Sawdust and Tinsel* is less unrelenting, problems are soluble, crises may be overcome.

The Face

According to Bergman, in an interview with Charles Thomas Samuels, *The Face (Ansiktet)* unconsciously 'corrects' *Sawdust and Tinsel*. The same might be said of *Winter Light* to its companion piece *Through a Glass Darkly*, or of *A Passion* to *Shame*. Yet, like all Bergman films, this particular depiction of the artist's plight forges its own distinctive identity. Certainly, the themes of journey, pretence and humiliation – as well as the opening shot of a coach silhouetted by a lonely skyline – recall *Sawdust and Tinsel*, whilst the closest subsequent parallel to *The Face* is *The Rite* which was made originally for television and offers similar content within tighter visual and dramatic bounds. *The Rite* also concerns the self-defence of an artistic troupe under judicial scrutiny but portrays only four characters and uses a single location; it is shot invariably in middle and full close-up. This overall compactness makes the film particularly suited for television, although both are black comedies and Bergman's comments on *The Rite* – 'they're artists on the way out' and 'between their profession and death they possess nothing' (*Bergman on Bergman*, p. 238) – apply to *The Face*, the crucial difference being that in *The Face* the defendants retain two invaluable qualities: self-confidence and perseverance.

In a plot possibly indebted to Chesterton's *Magic*, which Bergman produced in Gothenburg in 1947, the mesmerist Albert Emanuel Vogler and his cohorts head for work in Stockholm although down on their luck through widespread harassment. Passing through a forest they encounter a dying actor, Spegel, whom they take along but who dies shortly after disappearing from the scene on arrival at the city toll bar, where the troupe is escorted into a large house. Their host is Consul Egerman; also present are the royal medical consultant Vergerus and Starbeck, chief of

police. After formal introductions, Vergerus leads his fellow officials in an interrogation and examination of the 'dumb' Vogler,
concluding that he is a harmless charlatan. They offer the troupe a
performance permit in exchange for a private show the following
morning. The performance goes ahead, so scaring the coachman
Antonsson that he tries to strangle Vogler before hanging himself.
Vergerus pronounces Vogler dead, proceeding to erect an autopsy
table in the attic. Meanwhile Vogler, fooling the onlookers,
replaces himself with the now-deceased and suitably disguised
Spegel. Hiding in the attic, Vogler 'haunts' Vergerus to the point
of the physician's collapse. The troupe prepares a hasty departure
but Starbeck arrives, summoning Vogler upstairs. Expecting
arrest, the penniless mesmerist is, to his delighted surprise,
requested to perform for the king; sweeping out of sight of the
flabbergasted officials, 'Albert Emanuel Vogler makes his triumphant entrance into the Royal Palace'.

Although set in 1846, *The Face* relates equally to present day
crises of artistic means. Such contemporary relevance informs other
Bergman period pieces like *Sawdust and Tinsel, The Seventh Seal* and
The Virgin Spring, where specific dilemmas lead to meditations on
universal moral and philosophical themes. The choice of the mid-
nineteenth century offers Bergman a particularly dramatic confrontation between the claims of art and science. The Darwinian
era saw much pseudo-scientific virtuosity that thrived on a sceptical climate and a gullible public.

Vogler is a disciple of Mesmer, the founder of the science of
animal magnetism; like the name 'Magnetic Health Theatre',
Vogler synthesizes serious and frivolous elements. He is both
therapist and entertainer, a civilized medicine-man, a tribal
priest-performer in an increasingly materialistic age. His silent
response to official questioning and the ultimate intercession of a
father figure invite a Christian interpretation of Vogler. This loses
force, however, in the light of his reluctant but calculated corrupt-
ness; Vogler apparently succumbs to the mercenary influence of his
grandmother and his sidekick Tubal. An artist, like Albert in
Sawdust and Tinsel, walking an endless tightrope between destitu-
tion and wild success, Vogler turns 'vaudevillian', benefiting from

a technique which we know, from Dickens and Strindberg, fascinated the Victorian mind. Vogler's studied muteness protects him against the incisive analysis of legal-scientific procedure, a subversive stance which disturbs his critics. In this respect, it resembles the unequivocal stubborn silence of Elisabet Vogler in *Persona*, driving her practical young nurse to hysteria. Both actress and mesmerist, whose common surname seems more than coincidental, conveniently choose silence in order to play subtly desperate games, ironically in reaction to, but by the devices of, their professional lives.

Bergman's strategic image is that of the face as mask, whether the double face of Vogler's public and private life, or his wife Manda's impersonation of Aman (a-man), or the similar, stereotypical faces of the opposition and servants: Starbeck, bloated and officious; Egerman, genteel but ineffectual; Vergerus, prim and precise – and so on, down to the laconic brutishness of Antonsson, to whom the terrified footman Rustan remarks:

> There is something special about those faces. Do you understand what I mean? ... One ought to trample them. Faces like Vogler's and Aman's and the old woman's ...
>
> (*Four Screenplays*, p. 285)

Spegel and the old woman (Granny) also possess the enigmatic face – 'a shadow of a shadow' – which clouds identity and causes alarm. Spegel ('mirror' in Swedish) reflects Vogler's transformations; immediately seeing through Vogler's disguise, he is the only stranger unimpressed by the mesmerist's act. A formerly renowned actor gone to seed, a disintegrating man of talent, he foreshadows Winkelman in *A Passion*, who also wanders drunk in the woods. Like Vogler, Spegel is an illusionist and it remains unclear whether he reappears in Vogler's shadowy bed chamber as a living person or merely spectral brandy-thief and axe-wielder. Spegel functions partially to remind the spectator that the question of perceptual truth hangs over not only this particular plot but also the cinematic experience as a whole, a theme developed more self-consciously and extensively in *Persona*. When Spegel asks Vogler if he is 'a swindler who must hide his real face' (p. 250), Vogler's retort is sudden laughter, anticipating Elisabet's Vogler's initial reaction to the onstage loss of speech that precipitates her breakdown in *Persona*.

Spegel also detects Manda's disguise, noticing that 'he' is reading a book about cardsharps and asking, ironically, 'Colleagues, then?', to which Tubal's curt 'no cardsharps here' elicits laughter from the actor. Yet neither Spegel, Vogler, nor associates can fathom the depth of Granny's face. Whereas Vogler contrives his supernatural feats, Granny suggests more realistic powers. At the necromantic extreme of magic, her firm belief in amulets, omens and incantations relates her more to a time, of *The Seventh Seal* for instance, when superstition held sway. Vogler's 'occultism' is that of a modern entertainer, whose act relies on naive scientism and mechanical apparatus. In spite of her anachronistic image, Granny is no less of a poseur than Vogler – witness her peddling of false remedies in the kitchen. Indeed, Vogler is much less successful financially than Granny, who eventually admits to hoarding a fortune and leaves the impoverished troupe to go her own way. Bergman thus avoids making Granny a medieval stereotype, although it seems equally unlikely that her enigmatic role veils a mouthpiece of divine wisdom or 'God-dynamic' in the film, as Arthur Gibson supposes. Vernon Young suggests more appropriately that she may symbolize *decaying* religion and Vogler decaying art.

The film, then, portrays the artist as proffering an imitation or embellishment of reality, whereas Vogler's critics stand not only for rationalist doubt but also bourgeois conformity and authoritarianism. Hence an additional distinction from Vogler who, like Albert in *Sawdust and Tinsel*, is granted no social status and is considered a semi-vagrant outsider. Yet Vogler is no more socially spurious than any of his opponents with their nervous, mannered veneer. Vogler and his team show genuine amazement when Egerman directs them to the kitchen for supper; their world knows no such stratification. The critics' solidarity is, in any case, superficial: Starbeck is a parvenu, uncomfortable in the company of his fellow investigators; Vergerus' nocturnal overtures to Manda belie his propriety; Egerman is a hypocrite, confessing a belief in the supernatural but allowing his social role to excise any latent sympathy for his guests. Only Ottilia Egerman protests the examination and confides in Vogler; overhearing this, her jealous husband forces her to endure his 'proper' show of strength.

The widening gap between the Egermans, increased by Ottilia's loss of her child, comes across poignantly in the bedroom scene during the afternoon. Scared yet fascinated by Vogler's powers, they fail to communicate with each other at the time of their greatest need. Vergerus pretends to be unafraid of Vogler but Ottilia detects his uneasiness. Vogler fools his master tormentor into believing that 'there is no doubt that the man is dead' (p. 305) then, in the attic, into doubting his own terrified mind and admitting the possibility of sleeping when he thought he was awake. Vergerus is the progenitor of three similarly named specialists: the cynically methodical architect/photographer Elis in *A Passion*, the complacent doctor Andreas in *The Touch*, and the proto-Nazi experimenter Hans, in *The Serpent's Egg (Ormens Ägg)*. Bergman, however, is not altogether unsympathetic to Vergerus – 'the only completely integrated man in the film' – admiring his scepticism and passionate, obsessive involvement in his field.

In the name of scientific truth, Vergerus cross-examines Vogler rigorously in front of Starbeck, the Egermans and the mesmerist's colleagues. The enraged Vogler remains silent, baffling the physician. For Vergerus, who believes that 'it would be a catastrophe if scientists were suddenly forced to accept the inexplicable' (p. 266), Vogler's inscrutability admits to a truth beyond human understanding, the possibility of God, an idea thoroughly unwelcome to the physician. Unable to establish the 'truth', the examination becomes an exercise in humiliation, which Ottilia denounces in vain. It takes the form of a sadistic ritual: 'to humiliate and be humiliated ... is a crucial element in our whole social structure' (*Bergman on Bergman*, p. 81). Vogler's very existence repudiates the empirical values so dear to Vergerus, who counters with needless aggression. When religion and science both fail to offer certainty, does truth exist at all? For Spegel, 'truth is made to order; the most skilful liar creates the most useful truth' (p. 252), whereas for Manda 'nothing is true' (p. 293).

Although Vergerus forces Manda to admit the troupe's duplicity, his satisfaction is shortlived; Vogler's persistent silence ultimately turns to his advantage, contributing ironically to his revenge against Vergerus. Starbeck, royal proclamation in hand, asks Vogler to identify himself but fails to get a reply. Vergerus answers for him, unwittingly validating Vogler's right to royal patronage. For once, Vogler's brooding expression gives way to a sardonic, victorious smile; he rubs salt in his opponents' wounds by choosing to speak — authoritatively to a now obsequious Starbeck:

> Gather the rest of the apparatus and send it to the palace. Be careful; they are expensive objects (p. 324).

The artist regains his nerve; the showman wins out.

The inability of either faction to demonstrate a truthful reality (although Vogler's truth is a matter of expediency) defines both style and structure of *The Face*. Subtitled 'A Comedy', it presents nonetheless an uneven mixture of elements. Bergman states that the film is 'not to be taken seriously' but agrees that it turned out blacker than intended, pointing out that at the time he identified very much with the impecunious and misunderstood Vogler and adding that he then received a grant, an unexpected improvement in fortune similar to the mesmerist's. In the final sequence, the sun comes out suddenly after rain, contrasting with the general shadowy, portentous tone of the film. As in *Wild Strawberries*, an oscillation between sun and storm pertains to the changing fortunes of the characters. The ominous calm of the summer evening in the woods is a prelude to tragedy as in *Summer Interlude, The Seventh Seal* and *Through a Glass Darkly*. Clocks and bells again play their part in creating a mood of tension; weary sunlight and steady ticking combine in the afternoon hiatus to create an atmosphere of emptiness around the restless Egermans.

The attic scene is a gothic tour de force, disproportionate to the whole in Robin Wood's view, yet powerfully articulating Vogler's subtle method of revenge and allowing the dominant image — of the face — to appear in the huge mirror, seemingly afloat around Vergerus in the semi-darkness. A dummy run for *Hour of the Wolf* perhaps, but no more of a cliché than the below-stairs sub-plot, which at least underlines the overwhelming presence of the super-natural and heightens the social contrast. The domestic warmth cannot however eliminate the pervasive doubt and fear from the minds of the maid Sinna, the manservants and Tubal – reminiscent of Frid in *Smiles of a Summer Night* and the squire in *The Seventh Seal* – who wants out and gets it.

We recall that Bergman's childhood fascination with film began with his acquisition of a primitive episcope; the image of Vogler's magic lantern distinguishes *The Face*, not only as a highly sensitive personal statement about the ambiguous identity of the artist and his relationship with a hostile public, but also as a reminder of the genesis of Bergman's own career.

Hour of the Wolf

The most horrific, the most cruelly masochistic of all Bergman's 'portraits of the artist' is *Hour of the Wolf*, yet another case-study in creative despair. A painter, Johan Borg, and his wife, Alma, arrive by boat on a lonely island. During their stay, Johan falls prey to paranoid hallucinations, caused in part by his conscience plaguing him with a sense of his unimportance as an artist. He becomes taciturn, fearing contact with a world bent on his destruction, even rebuffing his unselfish wife, as he sinks into private fantasies. Communication, of any kind, is at a premium; the opening sequence firmly establishes this pervasive silence, with the noise-less arrival of their boat. Johan's crisis point is a drawn-out 'hour of the wolf' – the last hour of total darkness, when, he claims, most births and deaths occur. The deadly silence of this scene, where a terrified Johan strikes match after match to pass the time, epitom-izes Bergman's naturalistic style. A Hoffmann-inspired gothicism dominates the latter part of the film, when Johan enters a castle inhabited by his 'demons'. The visual expressionism of this super-natural episode gives the film a fascinatingly hybrid quality: it is as if, imagistically, *Through a Glass Darkly* combines with *The Silence*.

The debt to E.T.A. Hoffman is quite deliberately emphasized

throughout the film: the names of several characters are taken from his works, such as Kreisler the 'kappelmeister', Heerbrand the curator, and Lindhorst the archivist (*Bergman on Bergman*, p. 218). Poe and Almqvist are two other strong influences, and behind them all, the omnipresent Strindberg: as a study of an artist's neuroses, *Hour of the Wolf* is Bergman's version of his great precursor's *Inferno*. But there are also more personal sources of great potency: Bergman has said that he is, and always has been, frightened of birds, and a crucial scene in *Hour of the Wolf* shows Max von Sydow attacked by a flock of them. The horror of a darkness haunted by demons can probably be traced back to when, as a child, Ingmar Bergman used to be punished by being shut up in a wardrobe or small cupboard, where he imagined that a small creature was trying to bite off his toes.

There are significant parallels, too, between Mozart's *Magic Flute* (which Bergman has directed for the stage and television) and *Hour of the Wolf*; firstly, Tamino's search for Pamina and his quest for happiness and the ideal are similar to Johan's own longing for unattainable peace and reconciliation to his situation; secondly, the trials Tamino goes through parallel Johan's own ordeals, specifically the sequence leading up to the ultimate sexual humiliation with Veronica Vogler. But, as Robin Wood astutely observes, 'the relationship of Bergman's film to Mozart's opera is complex and important, containing at once a terrible irony and a positive assertion beyond irony's reach' (p. 162); the negative aspects of the movie, in other words, are tempered to some extent by the positive impulse of the opera to which it makes homage.

The script is based on a revision of another text, written for a projected film which pre-dated *Persona* and was to have been called *The Cannibals*. It was never made, but the expression 'cannibals' and the general conception clearly survive in the definitive version which shows the progression towards final and complete breakdown in Johan Borg. The breakdown is caused by an inability to resolve the dilemma posed by the situation of the artist in society, together with an inability to cope with tensions within the artist's own psyche and the horrors lying within his unconscious. The film holds out no hope for the reconciliation of the artist to the world:

Johan is entirely overwhelmed by the situation in which he finds himself, one which invites later comparison with *Persona* in respect of the confusion between reality and fantasy, and of the breakdown of identity and the schizophrenic state which Johan suffers.

The unconscious terrors are personified within the film as the inhabitants of the castle. Robin Wood suggests that these personifications are non-specific, but the Baron could equally be interpreted as representing the philistine and patronizing public's attitude to the artist (as in the story he tells Johan at the dinnerparty about deliberately hanging a picture upside-down and inviting its painter to see it). Similarly the old woman may represent the ugly side of sexuality, or sexuality as seen through the filter of Lutheran repression and guilt, and the homosexual pest seems an obvious projection of Johan's own possible latent homosexuality, which surfaces in the sequence of the boy's murder.

The 'portrait of the artist' which the film delineates is summed up by Johan's remarks at the excruciating dinner party, and has been put by Bergman himself in an interview. This portrait is the opposite of the comfortable and romantic view: it depicts, rather, 'unending torment, toothache', and in no sense implies that his is a gift from on high implying an other-worldly relationship. It resembles more a disease, a perversion, a 'five-legged calf' (*Bergman on Bergman*, p. 219); it is a brutal situation. The artist – as Beckett, decades before, stressed in his study of Proust – is compelled willy-nilly to create, however hopeless, oppressive and repulsive the task. If he is moderately fortunate, the artist can hope to give the abortion his psyche has spawned what Bergman calls 'professional form' and even earn his living through it; if he is not successful in taming his demons, however, he will end up insane like Johan Borg.

In the course of the film Borg becomes isolated not only from society but also from his personal world, in particular from his loving, fecund wife Alma, in whose devotion to him there might have been some hope of reconciliation to the world. At the end of the film she says hopelessly: 'If only I could have been with him all the time', that is mentally and emotionally as well as physically present. She herself – the firm, stable focus of the film's tensions, its sheet anchor, the measure of reality against which the horrific distortions provoked·by the other characters are judged – represents a current of sanity and integrity. Her pregnancy is the film's only symbol of hope and Johan's case is shown to be desperate when he withdraws from her, and from the world she inhabits.

The film as a whole represents the 'hour of the wolf' in Johan's life – the approach to, and arrival at, his psychological nadir. The sequence of the 'hour of the wolf' itself is the final break in the Alma/Johan relationship; he begins to see her too as a 'demon' and it is at this point that he tries to shoot her. However, it is not at this point where his doom is clearly set out. There is still the hope that this mad act might bring him to his senses. However, his fate is sealed when Johan accepts the invitation to the dinner party at the castle, thereby putting himself at the mercy of his 'demons'. This is in contrast to the scene in which he strikes down the demon-figure who persists in following him along the path to the cottage from the location where he had been painting (a way of representing resistance to his unconscious horrors).

Robin Wood's interpretation of these events is almost exclusively based on Freudian concepts. In the interview with Bergman referred to earlier, Torsten Manns suggests more plausibly, however, a Jungian basis for the film's imagery and symbolism, especially for the murder of the boy, shot (like the guilt-ridden meeting with Veronica Vogler on the beach) in over-exposure. It is too simple to regard this sequence as merely an expression of suppressed inclinations to pederasty. The boy attacks Johan by biting him; he concentrates in his person, with grotesque but revealing appropriateness, all the forces threatening Johan's sanity. When his murdered body refuses to sink, this is not simply an avowal of homosexual tendencies which refuse to be repressed, but more of the resistance of neuroses to cure. Just as the boy cannot drown, Johan's demons will not disappear. The notion that Bergman is handling a universal phenomemon with applications outside his own situation is more attractive – and more plausible – than a straightforward analysis of the film as a Freudian projection of conflicts within the director himself. The castle is a symbol of the unconscious – the collective unconscious – and its inhabitants are

figures of the influences inhabiting it. The demons which destroy
Borg are for all that non-existent outside his own mind; they are, as
Eric Rhode says, 'monstrous dissociations of dream' (*The Listener*,
18 July 1968). Johan destroys himself: not deliberately, but
inevitably and without power to resist.

This beautiful and macabre film, showing faces dissolving into
skull-like shapes, the death's-head showing through beneath the
skin, and featuring the artist as a 'grotesque demonic clown',
reveals, as Robin Wood aptly puts it, a 'freer human being' at
work, drawing upon a popular and familiar tradition of horror to an
extent which depersonalizes the horror. The result is a work of
great subtlety and ambiguity, a film of real, if sombre, humour: a
moving and fitting conclusion to Bergman's repeated efforts at
sketching in film the portrait of the artist as showman, as moun-
tebank, and as universal dreamer of our nightmares and scapegoat
for our sins.

A Film Trilogy

Through a Glass Darkly

Bergman refers to the theme of his trilogy, in which *Through a
Glass Darkly* is the first film, as a metaphysical 'reduction' –
leading in this case to 'certainty achieved.' Yet the film demonstrates that such certainty, if at all valid, depends on a number of
intellectual and dramaturgical compromises by the director.
Indeed, the peculiarities of the film bear out the fact that a trilogy
as such existed only after the completion of all three pieces over a
two-year period. Moreover, in its critical examination of the artistic personality, *Through a Glass Darkly* follows *The Face*, the major
changes lying in Bergman's attitude towards the artist, the question of God's existence, and his own cinematic style. We see the
artist in a less sympathetic light, sense an increasing theological
scepticism, and notice an unprecedented compositional austerity.

The film tells of the schizophrenic breakdown of a young woman
(Karin), married to a doctor (Martin) and staying at the island

home of her widowed father (David) and younger brother (Minus). Karin's derangement leads her to believe that God will emerge from the wall of a disused upstairs bedroom and also that she is able to penetrate the wallpaper and enter the 'world' which lies behind. This links the film to *Prison*, in which Birgitta-Carolina is confronted by a mad painter who gets her to watch the play of sunlight on patterned wallpaper. Although Bergman eventually cut this incident from the finished film, he evidently retained the idea; the original title of *Through a Glass Darkly* was *The Wallpaper*. Bergman has said that the film reflects his immersion in music at the time, and that it was influenced by his production (at the Royal Dramatic Theatre in Stockholm) of Chekhov's *The Seagull*, with which there are distinct parallels. The film ends with Karin's total collapse, subsequent sedation and departure by helicopter for apparently permanent admission to a mental hospital.

In *The Face*, Bergman implies defence of the artistic vocation by seeming to side with his persecuted mesmerist. In *Through a Glass Darkly* he turns the tables. The 'artist' is David, a hack novelist with delusions of grandeur. The film sustains a bitter critique of his occupation, personality and ethics, clearly referring to some extent to Bergman himself. Indeed, he hints at this in a scene where David dons beret and old leather jacket, the director's own favourite on-set garments. Moreover, Vilgot Sjöman says of Bergman:

> All that is noticeable is the labour it means for him to write: he practically whines with the boredom of it ...
> [feeling] a pedantic need for clarity, which drives him to dryness; a lyrical suggestion he can handle much better in pictures than in language.
>
> (*Diary from a Bergman Film*, in *Sweden Writes*,
> Stockholm, 1965)

This struggle with language is David's major headache. The harder he strives for evocative phrases, the more frustrated he becomes and eventually opts for simple alternatives:

DAVID (reads): She came toward him, panting with
              expectation, scarlet-faced in the keen

wind ... (sighs) Oh my God, oh my
God.

He thrusts his spectacles up on his brow and hides his
grey face in his hands. But after a few moments he
resumes work.

DAVID (reads): She came toward him, panting with
expectation ...

He runs a long thin line through the rest of the sentence, and contemplates his work. Then he strikes out
all the rest, too.

DAVID: She came running toward him, her face scarlet
in the keen wind ...

He shakes his head and leans forward over his sheets of
paper, and in capital letters, in red ink, writes the
following: SHE CAME RUNNING TOWARD HIM.
Then he gives a sigh, shakes his head, runs a thick line
through what he had written in capital letters and
resolutely writes: 'They met on the beach.'

(*A Film Trilogy*, pp. 33-4)

His dilemma is the gap between the desire for inspiration and the
unsatisfactoriness of articulation, an idea expressed fluently by
Eliot in 'East Coker':

Trying to learn to use words, and every attempt
Is a wholly new start, and a different kind of failure
Because one has only learnt to get the better of words
For the thing one no longer has to say, or the way in
which
One is no longer disposed to say it. And so each venture
Is a new beginning, a raid on the inarticulate
With shabby equipment always deteriorating
In the general mass of imprecision of feeling,
Undisciplined squads of emotion.

David suffers from literary 'torments' and 'hateful words'; this idea
of language as hostile and alienating reaches a climax in *The Silence*
and *Persona*. The similarity to *The Seagull* also springs to mind:

Stills from *Through a Glass Darkly*

David's tribulations resemble those of Chekhov's two writers – the reputable Trigorin and the aspiring young Treplev. Trigorin's response to naive adulation of his work is 'As soon as it appears in print, I can't bear it, I see that it's all wrong,' while Treplev scratches out his 'banal' expressions in a scene very close to David's battle with the beach scene.

From a personal point of view, David's overriding fault is that his professional life preoccupies him. His family comes a very poor second to his work; he spends much of his time away from home and, having just finished a novel in Switzerland, plans to leave again soon for Yugoslavia. His thorough egotism causes a desperate restlessness – rather like that of the equally self-centred archaeologist, David Kovac, in *The Touch* – and an uneasy conscience, with which he is forced to come to terms as he witnesses his daughter's mental disintegration. His personal crisis is precipitated by Karin's discovery of his diary, in which he admits to an obsessive exploitation of people as potential subject-matter:

> Her illness is hopeless, with occasional improvements. I have long suspected it, but the certainty, even so, is almost unbearable. To my horror, I note my own curiosity. The impulse to register its course, to note concisely her gradual dissolution. To make use of her.
>
> (*A Film Trilogy*, p. 35)

This not only anticipates the discovery, also in writing, of Elisabet Vogler's similar attitude to her nurse in *Persona* but also relates to Trigorin's remark: 'I catch up every word and phrase we utter, and lock them in my literary stockroom – they may be useful.' Trigorin, like David, cannot escape from his role – 'Day and night I am haunted by one thought. I must write, I must write' – though Trigorin at least feels that his activity stems from a duty to write about Russia and its people, whereas David's 'situational banalities' are invariably melodramatic and unidimensional.

David, like Borg in *Wild Strawberries*, is driven to a change of heart, shown in his remark to Karin after he has asked her to forgive his selfishness: 'When I think of all the lives I've sacrificed to my so-called art, it makes me sick' (p. 53); it is like Trigorin's painful realization that 'life and science keep moving farther . . . ahead . . . and, in the end, I feel that I only know how to paint landscapes and in all the rest I am false . . .' David finally sacrifices his art out of love for his family. If he is to make amends to his lost daughter and confused, distressed son, he must put other things out of his mind, so 'methodically, he feeds bundle after bundle of the typewritten sheets into the flames' (p. 55); it resembles Treplev's decision to tear up all his manuscripts after the departure of his love, Nina.

David's metamorphosis – overdone in the end – is not just self-induced, but owes much to both overt and covert criticism from Martin and Minus respectively. Martin is an academic, a medical lecturer at a Polytechnic. His feet planted firmly in a scientific world, he tells David a few home truths. At first he is ironic – 'I felt I had to drop you a line. Even if it disturbed you in the very act of creation' (p. 17) – later, with Karin declining, quite blunt: 'the worst of it is your lies are so refined, they resemble truth' (p. 46) and, echoing Sara's damning remarks to her cousin in *Wild Strawberries*, 'There's only *one* phenomenon you haven't an inkling of: life itself' (p. 45). Minus realizes that David is a mediocre writer and unaware of the fact. It upsets him that his father is so distant, as he tells Karin: 'Think, if for just once in my life I could talk to Daddy. But he's so absorbed in his own affairs' (p. 22).

In a sequence comparable to the first act of *The Seagull*, Minus, Karin and Martin enact a short play, written by Minus and performed in honour of David's return. The stage is a crudely built structure in the garden. The piece is highly ironic, intentionally so, it would seem, for Martin announces it as 'a morality play, intended only for poets and authors' (p. 25). Minus presents himself as a purist, not content with 'the completed work, banal fruit of simple-minded strivings' (p. 26) but concerned, in Mallarméan style, with the great work that will never be written. Holding this 'mirror' up to David hurts him deeply, although he refuses to show it. Also, the failure of Minus to consummate his love for Karin, the 'Princess', ironically prefigures their unfortunate act of mutual consolation towards the end of the film. From the outset, Bergman reveals Minus' adolescent sexual complex; in spite of mutual trust and what amounts at times to a near-telepathic understanding between brother and sister, their relationship explodes into physical intimacy under the stress of Karin's sickness.

Karin confides in Minus, explaining to him her experience of the 'other' reality. Her unbalanced state renders her acutely aware of perceptual phenomena: for instance, sudden noises like thunderclaps or the screech of gulls deeply disturb her, while her hallucinations in the bedroom show her visual hypersensitivity. The 'other' reality manifests itself as imminent divine revelation, eventually taking the form of a large spider, filling Karin with horror. Bergman also describes the helicopter that comes for Karin as 'a gigantic dark insect,' its shadow sweeping across the house moments before her traumatic vision. The helicopter clearly suggests Karin's abduction by a malignant God but, like the rest of the denouement, this comes over as facile, heavy-handed and all too convenient from a dramatic standpoint. Nevertheless, Bergman's doubt of the Christian God really begins at this stage – 'something destructive and fanatically dangerous' – leading, in *Winter Light*, to grave doubt of the existence of God in any form whatsoever.

The upshot of the tragedy is David's rather unconvincing assertion that 'God is love' and Minus' equally premature exclamation of relief that 'Daddy spoke to me.' Indeed, the film is less concerned at root with God's presence or absence than with human love or, rather, the tragic lack of it. The end of the film offers an easy solution to a metaphysical problem at the very time when answers were rapidly disappearing from Bergman's sight. This anomaly justifies our suspicion of the optimistic coda, in which David and Minus reassert themselves without much apparent difficulty. Bergman admits the faults of the film: general theatricality ('a surreptitious stage-play'), forced directorial control ('gewollt'), and emotional dishonesty. In the final analysis, it is a stiff drama redeemed only by occasional cultural and psychological insights.

But, for all its weaknesses, *Through a Glass Darkly* is notable in two distinct but interrelated areas: setting and natural sound. The film establishes the sea as a pervasive Bergman image, and while both *Winter Light* and *The Silence* are set inland, they deal with equally isolated locations. It is noteworthy that Bergman shot *Through a Glass Darkly* on the island of Gotland – adjacent to his subsequent home and location on Fårö, backdrop to such films as *Hour of the Wolf*, *Shame* and *A Passion*. The photography captures the bleakness of this environment, so that even if Bergman's 'reduction' theme disappoints with regard to plot, it receives striking visual definition in the sparse imagery. The lonely coastline, shot in limpid black and white, supports the stormy, threatening atmosphere of the film, symbolized by the early shot of a lighthouse beaming its recurrent warning. Oscillations in the weather have the same function here as in *Wild Strawberries* or *The Face*, only now – and frequently henceforth – we come to associate the austere surroundings with the despair and alienation of their solitary, sea-bound inhabitants, who draw, as David acknowledges, 'a magic circle around [themselves], shutting out everything that hasn't any place in one's own private little game' (p. 54).

Bergman allows his audience to realize the importance of natural sound by setting it in a context of 'damp, expectant silence.' There is one notably long, silent sequence: from the shots of David in his study at night through Karin's early morning wanderings, prompted by her inability to rest while sea birds are shrieking outside. The association of this sound with fear and despair puts one in mind of Faust in his palace in the second part of Goethe's play:

A bird will croak; croak what? Calamity.
Enmeshed by superstition, we're forlorn:
For things will happen, and forbode, and warn.
Frightened, we stand alone; our blood runs thin.
(tr. Walter Kaufmann)

Music follows Karin's discovery of David's diary – Bach's Suite No. 2 in D Minor for cello – but it is otherwise little used in the film. However, its rare employment gives it greater impact as an alternative to the pitfalls of language, as a sole remaining vehicle of truth and understanding. This function emerges fully in *The Silence*, when music by Bach becomes the only means of communication between the Timokan waiter and the travelling Swedes.

Before *Through a Glass Darkly*, natural sound — always something of a Bergman trademark — was generally incorporated into richer visual and musical fabrics. In this film, Bergman intensifies the drama by careful pinpointing of such everyday sounds as birdcall, feet on pebbles, foghorns, rainfall and the rattle of a milk churn. Within a framework of tense silence, these sounds stand out as landmarks of the characters' mental states — a form of low-key aural symbolism that works semi-consciously, relying to a large extent on the audience's power of association with certain prototypical psychic conditions. The noises are, therefore, as Claude Perrin points out in the issue of *Etudes cinématographiques* devoted to the trilogy, both objective and subjective at the same time, evoking both the material world and its emotional correlatives.

In the predominantly aural description of a wet afternoon (p. 50), we witness the possible genesis of a later Bergman film: 'like a cry and a whisper, the rain beats in fierce gusts against the window pane.' And now, indeed, we see through a glass, darkly.

Winter Light

Winter Light is a remarkable film in two respects: it not only rejects, albeit tentatively, a belief in God's existence for the first time in Bergman's career but also perfects his exercise in 'minimal' cinema. It presents a far more convincing metaphysical reduction than its predecessor. Although the unity of the trilogy is dubious — since *The Silence*, for all its thematic bleakness, reverts to more expressionistic imagery, and since several later films refine the 'minimal' style and notion of Godless solitude almost to breaking point — it does radically further Bergman's theological debate, moving from grandiose, last ditch vindications of faith through agnostic non-commitment to atheistic despair.

The film traces the personal crisis of a doubting priest, Tomas Ericsson, from hypocritical habit to total disillusionment. His dilemma reflects Bergman's desire for a 'showdown with an old concept of God' and an attempt to 'glimpse . . . a new, much more

difficult to capture, difficult to explain, difficult to describe God'
(in *Diary from a Bergman Film*). Tomas, like Isak Borg in *Wild
Strawberries*, is compelled to face his complacency, insincerity and
selfishness. Since the death of his wife, Tomas has become increasingly insecure, introspective and obsessed with the past. He tells
the suicidal fisherman, Jonas Persson, about his experience of the
Spanish Civil War: 'I refused to accept reality. I and my God lived
in one world, a specially arranged world, where everything made
sense' (*A Film Trilogy*, p. 84). He remains the same thirty years
later, still hiding behind the convenience of a faith that is slowly
collapsing, exposing his loneliness, his bogus priesthood and his
fear. He admits to Persson that he took orders to please his zealous
parents (shades of Bergman's background) and speaks of being
'well brought-up,' by which he means shielded from emotional
trauma or material hardship. His privileged status in the conservative, rural community is expressed ironically in a shot of a villager
leading a horse past Tomas – in the depths of his despair – and
doffing his hat respectfully to the priest.

Awareness of God's silence racks Tomas, who realizes the absurdity of his beliefs and discovers nothing beyond his ritual incantations. Alone in the deadened atmosphere of the church, he suffers
intensely, at one point echoing Christ's cry: 'God, my God, why
have you abandoned me?' Only by experiencing doubt and pain can
he learn the true meaning of godliness. It is a startling revelation.
As Bergman points out, in the course of his journey from
Mittsunda at matins to Frostnäs for evensong, Tomas follows
stations of his own cross. However, any such Christian identification must also account for Tomas' mistress (the schoolteacher,
Märta Lundberg) and the crippled sexton, Algot Frövik, whose
interpretation of Christ's Passion partially redeems the doubting
Tomas. Frövik is equally troubled by God's silence, believing that
Christ's real suffering lay in his awareness of this fact rather than in
his physical anguish. He reaches this conclusion by comparing
Christ's and his own agony, deciding that Christ's four hours were
preferable to his own continual pain.

Märta stands out as an atheist, concerned only with relating to
fellow beings, not to a faith which 'seemed ... obscure and

neurotic, in some way cruelly overcharged with emotion, primitive' (p. 81). Yet she wonders at Tomas's 'peculiar indifference to ... Jesus Christ' and – with eczema rashes as her stigmata and an overpowering desire to sacrifice her life for another (i.e. Tomas), as well as an apparent willingness to take his abuse and rejection in return for her avowal of love – emerges herself as a Christ-like figure. Tomas cannot bear Märta because she represents an overwhelmingly animal, practical existence. Moreover, he resents her attempt to replace his wife; her love letter to him ironically ends 'Dearest,' repeating Tomas' exclamation on looking at his wife's picture just before reading the letter. For Märta, Communion should be a 'love-feast' shared with Tomas. Her lack of pious awe offends and frightens him, because of his inadmissible envy of her. This ties in with Bergman's original theme, later abandoned: Tomas's envy of Christ. In the finished film this is modified to envy of a Christ figure, Märta (martyr).

Transitional events, like Persson's suicide and a confrontation with Märta at the schoolhouse, affect Tomas in the same way as Borg's painful memories in *Wild Strawberries*: they oblige him to consider others before himself. The two films also share brief but critical turning points: Tomas shuts the door on Märta but returns and invites her to accompany him to Frostnäs; on arrival there, Tomas makes a point of asking Frövik what he wanted to discuss at Mittsunda, when Tomas had curtly put him off. His gesture then prompts an insistent interpretation of Christ's Passion: that the loneliness at Gethsemene, the desertion of the disciples, Peter's denial, and Judas' betrayal, all serve to vindicate Tomas' suffering and offer a clue to the 'new ... difficult to describe God.'

The narrative movement from one parish to another is one way in which the film represents, as Robin Wood succinctly puts it, a general shift in the western world 'from religious orthodoxy ... [to] a kind of tentative existentialism' (p. 112). The rural location is important in this respect, portraying a community torn between its hierarchical traditions and a materialistic rootlessness which creates political fears of the kind that kills Persson. Wood puts it in a nutshell by saying that *Winter Light* is a 'spiritual documentary on contemporary Sweden' (p. 111); indeed, this contrast between

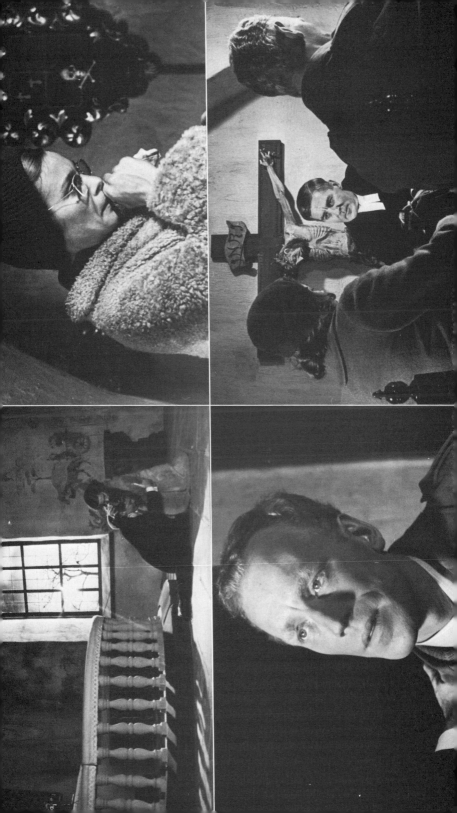

age-old isolation and modern patterns of communication consistently underlies the troubles of Bergman's more recent protagonists.

The hollowness of language relates closely to this web of what Wood calls 'cultural contradictions.' The opening sequence firmly establishes the breakdown of verbal communication. Tomas's expression betrays his mechanical, unfeeling incantation of the liturgy, while the long communion sequence noticeably lacks any speech apart from the priest's monotonous ministration and exclamations by Karin Persson ('tack', thank you, to Märta for helping her up from the communion rail) and Fru Apelblad who wakes her mischievous daughter. At one point, Märta calls words 'useless' and she is forced to correspond with Tomas in order to get through to him with the written word. Bergman presents her lengthy letter in full, which would undoubtedly be a cumbersome and distracting sequence if not for his superb front facial close-up of Märta, with a single cut-away flashback to vary the visual pace. The conversation between Tomas and the anxious Perssons is embarassingly inarticulate, full of repetition, awkward pauses and forced remarks:

TOMAS: You wished to speak to me.
MRS PERSSON: Yes. Though it wasn't quite like that
    either. It was Jonas, really, though he says nothing.
    So I thought . . . this morning I thought we'd come
    to church. And speak to someone else.
JONAS: We're at our wits' end.
MRS PERSSON: At our wits' end. (Nods) That's to say
    Jonas is. Not me so much. But Jonas is . . .
                                        (*A Film Trilogy*, p. 73)

Wood sees in it resemblances to Ionesco's work; indeed, much of the dialogue is reminiscent of those writers – like Pinter, Beckett, Arrabal, Sarraute – who focus on the ridiculous, superfluous and superficial nature of much of our speech.

Alone later with Persson, Tomas feels worthless and quite unable to help the fisherman, whose paralyzing fear of the Chinese and the atom bomb has driven him into a terrified withdrawal.

Seeing the reflection of his own alienation in the tense and taciturn
Persson, Tomas tries to escape by reversing the roles, thus trans-
ferring to Persson the responsibility of hearing a confession. He
tells his parishioner, ironically, 'We're all responsible; and we
must all take the consequences' (p. 83) – which Jan Rosenberg also
learns to his dismay in *Shame* – and speaks of their mutual betrayal
of 'the only condition under which men can live: to live together'
(p. 86). A further irony is that Tomas, like Evald in *Wild Strawberries*, appeals to the rationalist, anti-religious side of his simple
supplicant:

> TOMAS: Well, and what if God doesn't exist? What
>   difference does it make?
> JONAS: (looks towards the door).
> TOMAS: Life becomes something we can understand.
>   What a relief! And death – extinction, dissolution of
>   body and soul . . . You must live . . . Summer's on the
>   way . . . It's the earthly paradise . . .
>
> (p. 86)

There is also a curious parallel between the Tomas-Persson
relationship and that between Elisabet-Alma in *Persona*. A form of
personality transference takes place whereby Tomas, instead of
easing the pressure by universalizing the problem, only succeeds in
confirming Persson's worst suspicions; in place of comforting
words is a full-blown admission of faithlessness by the intended
counsellor. This additional burden proves too much for Persson
who, more frightened than ever, goes and shoots himself. The lack
of communication is further emphasized by an uneasy exchange
between Tomas and a boy who enters the schoolroom to collect a
comic book from his desk. While the scene might at first appear to
be a mere stopgap or break in the film's continuity, in fact it
confirms the growing gulf between priest and people, in particular
the irrelevance of religion to the younger generation.

The end of the film invites various interpretations, none of
which is totally satisfactory in view of its non-committal nature.
Although lacking a congregation, Tomas decides to hold evensong
but there is little or nothing in his tone of voice to suggest a

transformation. However, we may see an implicit optimism in a close-up of the brilliant chandelier which Frövik turns on to lighten the gloomy interior of the church. John Simon makes a triple classification of interpretations: Christian, nihilist and existentialist, with a preference for the latter. Yet for Bergman, the ultimate believer is Märta, who relieves Tomas of his burdensome struggle for faith. However, the service does take place at Tomas's bidding, possibly indicating a fresh start by the priest, or at least as Sjöman maintains, permitting 'a possibility of choice'. Bergman was evidently sensitive to the forced ending of his previous film, so the refusal to give an answer in *Winter Light* is not only the result of an insoluble problem but also his determination to avoid the type of facile denouement which mars *Through a Glass Darkly*; the organist Blom's cynical words to Märta – 'God is love, and love is God . . . I know the jargon' (p. 103) – reject David's belief out of hand. What is apparent is a need for human love and 'constant communion' between people to counteract the destructive tendencies in interpersonal relationships; above all, a need to persevere instead of succumbing to threat and fear: 'if God is silent you still have to go on with your work . . . Suddenly, one day, God answers, but it's your duty to go on' (Bergman, quoted by John Simon, p. 206).

Bergman says that *Winter Light* is the only one of his films that he really likes, where 'everything is exactly as I wanted to have it, in every second of this picture' (*Ingmar Bergman Directs*, p. 17). It is 'a settling of accounts' from *Through a Glass Darkly*, having both dramatic and thematic unity. It is one of Bergman's shortest features, running for only eighty minutes, compressing time more dramatically than any other Bergman film, reducing the relatively compact scales of *Sawdust and Tinsel*, *Wild Strawberries* and *The Face* to a mere three hours in a single day, from noon to three p. m. In this respect it approaches the correlation of film time to real time practised by such diverse film makers as Warhol, Hitchcock (in *Rope*), Varda (in *Cleo from Five to Seven*) and Michael Snow (in *Wavelength*).

Winter Light epitomizes 'minimal' cinema, its visual and aural bleakness corresponding perfectly to the severity of its subject matter. The whole film is set on a grey winter day, in conditions that cause the very landscape to seem peculiarly mute and static. In the main part of the church at Mittsunda, the light is consistently dull; in the vestry, one barred window admits a harsh light that almost sears Tomas in its intensity. Sven Nykvist, director of photography, describes the care with which he and Bergman dealt with the light, rendering it as naturalistic as possible, even though the interior shooting took place on a studio sound stage, utilizing in one shot only a candelabra and some fill-light. Their specific experiment with light was in deliberate reaction to the artificiality of modern high-speed photography. The accurate reproduction of the changing light over a three-hour period resulted from their exhaustive experiments with the then recently developed Eastman Double-X negative in a concerted effort to extend visual realism:

> We travelled around Dalecarlia, looked over some thirty churches located around Lake Siljan, and photo-graphed each one inside and out. Finally we chose Torsang church. We then gave this church intensive study during the number of cloudy days [in] September 1961 – and we observed particularly how the light changed inside the church from hour to hour. We recorded with a Leica camera the interiors at various times of day as the pattern of the light travelled through the empty old church. The resultant prints I pasted in my copy of the script ...
> (Nykvist, in *American Cinematographer*, October 1962)

Bergman's evocation of exterior landscape also shows remarkable fidelity to the numbing weather, as well as demonstrating his method of allowing individual images to reflect generally the mental states of the characters. One long shot stresses Tomas's utter alienation: he stands by Persson's body with cold, unmoving countryside around him. Later, he and Märta stop for a freight train at a crossing: the coffin-like wagons present a complex, indirect symbol of the passing of death and weight, while the rais-ing of the barrier is an image of release for Tomas. In the screen-play, Bergman elaborates this sequence, with Tomas relating a

childhood trauma caused by the threatening proximity of the
railway line (in this way recalling Lagerkvist's childhood story,
Guest of Reality). Yet these implications remain subservient to the
authentic observation of a November day, when, in the words of
Siegfried Kracauer:

> Natural objects ... are surrounded with a fringe of
> meanings liable to touch off various moods, emotions,
> runs of inarticulate thoughts; in other words, they have
> a theoretically unlimited number of psychological and
> mental correspondences.
>
> (*Theory of Film* p. 68)

A further distinguishing feature of *Winter Light* is Bergman's
alternation of natural sound with silence and long pauses. Silence
emerges on a basic psychological and structural level. As Michel
Estève points out, in the trilogy issue of *Etudes cinématographiques*,
silence accompanies the shots of all communicants together, the
crucifixion icons, the Persson family seen through a window after
learning of Jonas's death (Tomas looking in from outside, like Borg
in *Wild Strawberries*), and Jonas's corpse wrapped in a tarpaulin.
Music is evident to an even lesser degree than in *Through a Glass
Darkly*. We hear only the church organ and peal of bells, although
Bergman says that *A Psalm Symphony* by Stravinsky inspired the
film. This musical inspiration leads to a film in which, says Estève,
'the internal rhythm ... is created by silence, on the level of shot
and sequence'. Only natural sound emerges from the 'dead' landscape: footsteps on the stone floor of the church, the steady ticking
of a clock, the whinny of a horse, the purr of an idling car engine,
the roar of a weir. The screenplay coordinates thematic and atmospheric silence:

> No footsteps, no sound of a door closing. No wind in
> cracks and crevices. Complete silence. He drags himself
> over to the window.
> No car, no traces, Not a sound. The snow falls softly
> and steadily.

God's silence, Christ's twisted face, the blood on the
brow and hands ...

(p. 87)

The falling snow smothers all but isolated sound. It is a powerful
technique, enabling *Winter Light* to convey its nervous message not
merely by plot or dialogue but also by a multi-sensory experience
that seems to place the spectator in the actual cold, dark scene.

The Silence

> *Dawn points, and another day*
> *Prepares for heat and silence ...*
> (T.S. Eliot, *East Coker*)

We should not recoil from the suggestion that Bergman is theo-
logically rather naive. Even allowing for a lame translation, the
descriptive subtitles he has given the films of the trilogy are
simplistic. In the case of *The Silence*, it is stated to be about 'God's
silence – the negative impression'. We can accept the first half of
this – 'Guds tystnad' is heard, or more accurately felt, throughout
the Bergman canon, and not only in *The Seventh Seal* – but what can
possibly be meant by 'the negative impression'? If Bergman really
thinks that the first film of the trilogy demonstrates the 'achievement of certainty', the second its unmasking, and *The Silence* the
reverse of that impression of certainty, then we are up against yet
another instance of the artist's intention being at best a distraction
and at worst an irrelevance in the appraisal and exegesis of his
work. Of course, the silence of God is part of the meaning of *The
Silence* – but it doesn't by any means exhaust the resonance of this
extraordinary work, any more than the speculations of Vladimir
and Estragon about the number of thieves 'saved' with Jesus at
Golgotha provide a key to more than one – quite limited – aspect of
Beckett's play *Waiting for Godot*.

Not that we should – or can – neglect the 'philosophical'
concerns explored in the film. However, the technical aspects of
Bergman's achievement in *The Silence* are equally as important. In

an interview published in *Movie*, Bergman declared that the film afforded him the opportunity to 'break up' his own patterns, and 'go quite a different way' from the one he had been following before. In so doing, he added new images to the vocabulary of film, instead of, as hitherto, drawing on a pre-existing stock of imagery. In other words, whereas the iconography in Bergman's previous films owes a lot to the imagery of the major filmmakers (Renoir in particular), with *The Silence* he began to break fresh ground. One of the areas of cinematography affected was pace of cutting: this film is cut very slow, the *lenteur* contributing markedly to the overall atmosphere of oppressive and threatening calm. Bergman also continues to experiment with the sound-track: we hear only natural sounds, and music picked up on the radio; in the brilliant opening sequence the train carrying the sisters and Johan to the unfamiliar city slips silently along the rails, as if to emphasize the unreality combined with menace which the strange country represents to the travellers; and no footfalls are heard in the hotel.

A further departure was the paring down of the 'plot' to the bare minimum: the sisters arrive at a hotel, one of them gravely ill; the other picks up a local man (played mutely but powerfully by Birger Malmsten, who also appears in *Prison, Thirst, Summer Interlude* and Godard's *Masculin, féminin*); the sisters argue, and then separate; as the train carries Anna and Johan away, Johan reads the 'few words of the foreign language' which his aunt Ester has written out for him, words for things like spirit, fear and joy. Yet another innovation on Bergman's part was his decision to discard the somewhat overt symbolism of his earlier films – a symbolism which tended to draw attention to itself in favour of new and more personal, expressionistic images. The imagistic innovations, of course, cover the whole trilogy, although they tend to be of a different kind, for instance, the lighthouse at dusk in *Through a Glass Darkly* anticipating the mood-environment correlations in *Persona* and *A Passion*. The expressionism is novel, although not totally without precedent, as in the beach/bathing scene in *Sawdust and Tinsel*; quite a lot of the graphic symbolism in *Virgin Spring* is quasi-naturalistic, and in *The Seventh Seal* it is overtly allegorical. However, the dwarfs, or the armoured vehicles, when they crop up in the film, seem immediately less problematical than before, and at the same time more resonant for being open to a wider spectrum of interpretation. Likewise, the lighting in the film, although obviously symbolic, is less directly so than was the case in *Wild Strawberries*: here, for instance, we have the change from black to white in Anna's dress at the end; and in the corridors of the hotel, Johan casts no shadow. On another level of symbolism, there is the powerful effect of the parenthetic editing of the arrival and departure of the tank around Johan's Punch and Judy show.

Finally, there is the setting itself, a study in claustrophobia; the film is shot almost entirely in oppressive interiors, bedrooms, corridors, and compartments. Even the street is narrow; the café and the cinema visited by Anna are constricting. In face the whole film, at every level, takes a gamble with the medium, posing the question of how much it can jettison of old-fashioned devices and still survive. In so doing it evolves a new cinematic vocabulary – 'acting', as Bergman says (*Bergman on Bergman*, p. 181), 'by association; rhythmically, with themes and counter-themes' – which makes possible the later 'chamber films', especially *Persona, Hour of the Wolf* and *Cries and Whispers*.

As a result of these technical experiments in minimal cinema (minimal in terms of plot and location, the film being pictorially baroque and copious), we have in *The Silence* a film of oppressive power. It dwells long (and longingly) on a drab and dreary world, a world of aggressive heat and glare. Whereas, in *Winter Light*, the cold represents the paralysis of emotion, in *The Silence* heat compels the shedding of masks. Anna and Ester reach their moment of truth together when, clinging to her casual lover's embrace, Anna tells Ester: 'You can't live without your sense of your own importance ... You hate me, just like you hate yourself' (*A Film Trilogy*, p. 136). Against Ester's calm assertion that Anna is wrong, that she loves her, is hurled Anna's bleak and uncompromising question: 'Why do you live?' (compare the Ullmann/Thulin duo in *Cries and Whispers* – the seeds of all that is here). The world of *The Silence* is thus a world full of conflict, of aggression, of pity and comfort withheld; the isolation of the characters becomes more and more apparent as the film develops. It is an isolation within the confines of struggle, of spiritual loneliness, of a hell on earth. Perhaps the fact that Johan survives in his innocence, and that he carries with him his aunt's record of the words of the strange language, points to a note of hope: hope that the silence will not conquer and that language will survive. It is of note that Ester is a translator; that is, someone whose life is dedicated to ensuring the diffusion of works of the creative mind across the silencing barriers of language.

Ester and Anna represent two poles; the intellect and the senses. Ester is cool, even in the heat, while Anna sweats; Ester drinks; Anna likes food, Ester satisfies herself solitarily, her face in sexual ecstasy lit to look very like death, while Anna, inflamed by the frenzied coupling of the lovers she stumbles upon in the cinema, takes a man, she tells us, in a dark corner of a church. But neither temperament can grant itself peace. Ester, the 'mind', is tortured by a sick body; Anna, the 'body', is oppressed by shame and remorse at her erotic self-indulgence and her cruelty towards her sister. But once again all is not totally lost; as the train bears Johan and his mother away from Ester, Anna opens the compartment window and lets the rain splash regeneratively over her face and hands.

Although *The Silence* is a film of extreme starkness (despite the apparent light relief provided by the sinister antics of the dwarfs, who look like children but get drunk and cavort erotically like other adults), it can only be considered a 'boring' picture if spareness is held in itself to be monotonous. We are, it is true, unnerved by a movie that works to a time-scale close to the pace of life itself (like the frequent attention paid to clocks in *Cries and Whispers* and Bergman's reflective scanning of rooms and objects in emotionally charged sequences in his television films *Scenes from a Marriage* and *Face to Face*). Thus Ester's *ennui* is made palpable by the duration of its portrayal, and also by the fact that the camera moves in this film only with great economy. In fact economy is the keynote throughout: economy of gesture, of sentiment, of utterance, although the contrast of these economies with its pictorial richness gives the film a peculiar, challenging disunity. Not only is it shot in black and white, it is scripted with the bare minimum of dialogue: unlike

Stills from *The Silence*

Winter Light, where long dialogues show the difference between Tomas's articulate but inadequate speech on the one hand and the curt, semi-coherent sincerity of Persson and Märta's uncontrolled and pathetic effusions on the other.

Indeed, *The Silence* confronts the same problems as its predecessors, but unlike them it shows rather than states. What it shows is a bleak country of the soul, where joyless but compulsive eroticism reveals an essential sterility. It is not, like *Winter Light*, a film which for all its 'acoustic landscape' *talks* about God's silence; it is the representation of that silence. Whereas Bergman, *ancienne manière*, observed nothingness in the eyes of the young witch in *The Seventh Seal*, in this film he provokes direct experience of it. In *The Seventh Seal* we were told that God does not exist; in *The Silence* the death of God has become palpable, a matter of deep pain formulated not verbally but in the actions, expressions and gestures of the characters, of Ester choking on her bottle of brandy, of Anna pouting sensually and angrily, of Johan gazing helplessly at both of them. And whereas in *The Seventh Seal* the dialectic is conducted in the head, through language, here it is expressed physically, and operates directly upon our emotions.

It operates partly through unspecific but sharply-etched visual images, such as the military vehicles and the scraggy nag which passes by like a portent of doom, drawing a load of bric-a-brac. There are within the movie cases of subtle coincidence of imagery: for instance when Johan contemplates the baroque painting of a satyr abducting a not-too-unwilling nymph, an image followed not long afterwards by that of the erotic wrestling in the cinema stalls, and then of Anna's copulation with the café waiter.

And there are distinctive aural images, too. The script refers continually to the oppressive, tangible, even sticky quality of the silence in the town; and this is expressed on the soundtrack by sirens and bells and even the hard ticking of the clock which raucously shatters the stillness and invites it to reassert itself. There is even close juncture between verbal and visual expression. Ester speaks of her father, for instance; and the old waiter is shown acting paternally towards her. Perhaps it is this which gives her the strength to utter the most positive words in the film, words she gives to Johan just before he leaves: 'you must be brave ... you must be brave' (*A Film Trilogy*, p. 142).

Speaking of Ingmar Bergman in *The Times* (4 August 1973), the Swedish actress and director Mai Zetterling says, 'I think he's very close to being some sort of genius', and she singles out *The Silence* as being one of the films she most admires. But she states her unambiguous opposition to what he says, which she describes as 'very Lutheran and very agonized and very personal and sometimes very evil'. For an off-the-cuff reaction to an interviewer this is remarkably perceptive. Mai Zetterling not only notes the obvious things – the Protestantism, the anguish, the personal confession side of it – she also discerns an element of cruelty. In *The Silence* Bergman has made a film which is at one and the same time compassionate and cruel; he is taunting the dying Ester, but he is also comforting the neglected Johan; he is blaming God for refusing to speak, and yet sardonically belittling His attempts (as shown by Bergman himself) to do so. He is with Anna in her erotic frenzies, yet he is also with Ester in her revulsion at the 'fishy' odour of semen. Bergman clearly intends both to have his cake and to eat it. And, in *The Silence* at least, he gets away with it rather triumphantly.

Unserene Maturity

Persona

Bergman's dedication to an exploration of film as art relies on his feeling that it is nearing a discovery of its 'essential self'. This venture is like that of Rimbaud or Mallarmé seeking a perfect poetic form, so as to imply or even release the eloquent silence behind the word. For Bergman, as for those poets a century before, the film theorist Bela Balázs might have provided a motto: 'Silence is action ... and always an indication of some quite definite state of mind' (*Theory of the Film*, p. 226). *Persona* heralds a series of films in which a correlation of isolation and silence refers more to a secular than religious dilemma. *Persona* revolves around several related concepts of silence; going beyond *The Silence*, Bergman subjects the medium of film to radical examination. In so doing, he puts the whole notion of the cinema experience to the test.

Persona evolved from a script called 'The Cannibals', on which Bergman had been working until his illness in early 1966, and which ultimately manifests itself in *Hour of the Wolf*. This illness affected Bergman's hearing and eyesight, and to some extent his speech; his awareness of these symptoms clearly pertain to the audio-visual disruption and concept of silence in the film. *Persona* also introduces a theme which Bergman pursues in almost all of his subsequent films: a deep concern for the fate of the individual in a callous, selfish world, where suffering is both irrational and inevitable. Bergman depicts this anguish in a succession of localized actions, which unavoidably implicate his main characters in physical and mental violence.

The plot of *Persona* (in so far as one exists, in view of the narrative discontinuity) is about a 'sick' actress, Elisabet Vogler, and her young nurse, Alma. The ultimate effect of their vacation at a lonely summer cottage is the dissolution of their separate identities, and the apparent transference of personality from Elisabet to Alma. One may compare it to Beckett's novel *Molloy*, in which the heroes, Molloy and Moran, come to resemble each other, although they never meet. The closest parallel is that identification bears upon wish-fulfilment: by wanting to confront Molloy, Moran brings about his transmutation; by wanting to emulate her patient, Alma precipitates fusion with Elisabet. A comparison with Strindberg is more obvious: his play, *The Stronger*, involves two women in a drama of psychical domination and submission; further analogies may be drawn with *Creditors, Crime and Crime,* and *The Ghost Sonata*. Hoffmann is another likely influence: his novel *The Devil's Elixirs*, and stories, *Ritter Gluck* and *The Doubles*, among others, take up the themes of split personality and telepathic thought. In cinema, such ideas of transferred personality and mental possession also find expression in Losey's *The Servant*, Fassbinder's *Despair*, and Cammell/Roeg's *Performance*.

It is tempting but perfunctory to explain cases of personality transference from a psycho-analytic point of view. In any case, as

Susan Sontag points out, by including a psychiatrist's diagnosis early and late on in the published working draft, but dispensing with the second one in the film, Bergman dismisses the conclusions of medical psychology and opts for an open ending. The transference shows that, under pressure, the external self breaks down, crumbling the 'mask' which the individual wears for the benefit of society. Ibsen was strongly aware of this problem; in dramaturgy, 'persona' refers to the face-mask worn by an actor to project a particular type; ironically, the Greek word for hypocrite also signifies an actor: Norman O. Brown in *Love's Body* (p. 91), claims that 'sickness is all shamming, role-playing, acting out. And so is therapy'. In Jungian psychology – and John Simon says that Bergman was reading Jung at the time – 'persona' means a public 'face', the stripping away of which, according to Birgitta Steene, causes 'a state of mute unconsciousness; a human being stands face to face with his naked self (*Ingmar Bergman*, p. 115). This happens both to Elisabet and Alma, although in Alma's case, it follows on her own action. Although Elisabet seems passive throughout, Alma's recognition in herself of elements of Elisabet's psyche stimulates her involvement. Elisabet's unbroken silence causes Alma to lose control of her 'normal' self. The silence is catalytic yet, as Alma's false self is exposed, her loss of 'face' appears to be a natural occurrence.

In the first place, Alma radiates self-confidence and machine-like efficiency. She introduces herself concisely to Elisabet, showing herself to be socially and professionally appealing, a down-to-earth modern Swede. Her conventional personality contrasts sharply with Elisabet's highly-strung eccentricity. Alma's matter-of-fact speech is far removed from contrived stage speech – Elisabet's forte until, as Electra, she dried up during a performance and collapsed the following night. Her withdrawn state immediately shakes Alma's complacency. When the psychiatrist asks Alma for her initial impressions of the actress, the nurse replies, 'For a moment I thought I ought to refuse the job' (*Persona and Shame*, p. 26). Her conformity weakens her position: the psychiatrist knows that Alma will accept the summer-house assignment if it carries the promise of a special outfit 'or something equally

conservative and unpleasant' (p. 39). The transference is less a
strictly personal affair than the interaction (Elisabet as spiritual
artist, Alma as bourgeois materialist) of what Robin Wood calls
two 'representative consciousnesses'. It is more than Alma's professional interest that drives her to accept the task. She commits
herself firmly to nursing Elisabet, expressing a desire to get to the
root of the actress's trouble. She welcomes the task as a challenge to
the relative security of engagement and a hospital routine. By
becoming the addressee, when she reads Elisabet a letter from Mr
Vogler, Alma unwittingly prefigures her later identification with
the actress; at the same time, she gains insight into Elisabet's
private life.

In the seclusion of the summer cottage, Elisabet increasingly
fascinates Alma. The nurse, conscientious and enthusiastic,
becomes something of an amateur psychologist: 'she sends long
and detailed reports to the doctor' (p. 44). In a strange episode on
the beach, Elisabet takes Alma's hand and compares it with her
own. Alma hastily withdraws it, claiming that it is unlucky to
compare hands. This incident is highly ironic in view of the
imminent transference. The superficiality of Alma's self-
satisfaction is evident when she reads aloud to Elisabet, quoting a
passage which argues a loss of faith in religion, as a result of human
awareness of pain (a throwback to the trilogy). Alma now admits
problems of her own; Elisabet's silence goads her into growing
self-revelation: she gains an unsolicited confidante, an alluring
receptacle for her own misgivings. She tells Elisabet of her search
for a humanist substitute for religion. Alma slowly becomes a
patient while Elisabet, unconsciously perhaps, assumes the role of
therapist. As Alma releases her feelings, her mask cracks. All the
time, Elisabet keeps up a speechless attentiveness, concentrating
with a force which accelerates Alma's discomposure. Unaccus-
tomed to such receptiveness, she tries unavailingly to check her
slide, launching into a highly erotic account of a beach orgy. It is of
considerable significance that, in the film, Bergman utilizes no
flashback techniques, thus intensifying the stark retrospective
power of Alma's confession. It is also an example of Bergman's
belief in the camera as 'objective mediant' in excited, elaborate

Stills from *Persona*

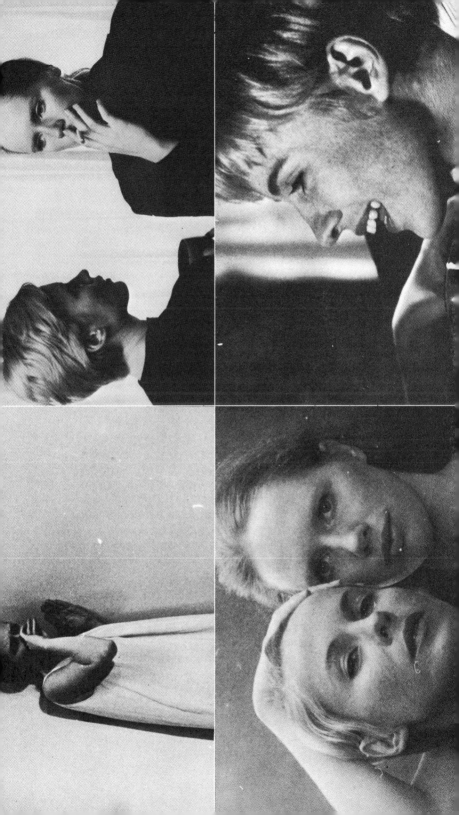

scenes. Towards the end of her recollection, Alma doubts Elisabet's
interest and envies her prolonged silence.

Their relationship deteriorates when Alma opens a woundingly
patronizing letter from Elisabet to her psychiatrist. Alma, bent on
revenge, spites Elisabet by allowing her to step on broken glass,
but it is a pyrrhic victory, as Elisabet reinforces her silence. Alma's
desperation reaches a point where she threatens to hurl boiling
water at Elisabet, and this at last elicits a terrified 'No!' from the
actress. A projector breakdown follows the glass sequence. It is a
shock tactic which Bergman allows as part of his method, disintegrating the image literally in front of the spectator's eyes. When the
drama resumes, the spectator's sense of security is as shattered as
Alma's. Thereafter, it is often difficult to distinguish reality from
fantasy; to spend time on a guessing game is as futile in *Persona* as it
is in Antonioni's *Blow Up*, which also questions the validity of
photographic images. Bergman effects a consistency – of doubt –
which reflects his acknowledged intention to extend interpretation
to the onlooker and renounce narrative omnipotence. By the time
a real/imaginary Mr Vogler appears, Alma has almost totally
absorbed her companion's personality. Vogler makes love to Alma,
unaware that she is not his wife, in spite of her denials. He persists
in addressing her as Elisabet, until she hears herself speaking with
'artificial tenderness'. In her schizophrenic state, Alma acts the
part of Elisabet; in an exalted, theatrical voice, she calls herself
mother of Elisabet's son. As Bengtsson, the colonel's servant in *The
Ghost Sonata*, says: 'When people stay a long time together and
torment each other they go mad'. Elisabet, witnessing this mental
takeover, realizes to her mortification that Alma is a better mother
than she has ever been.

During this episode in the film, the faces of the two women
merge until the image suggests a single face, half-Elisabet, half-
Alma (Bergman does this less pointedly in *Sawdust and Tinsel* and
Cries and Whispers). Alma censures Elisabet's failure in motherhood, her own voice 'confessing' for Elisabet. Bergman twice films
Alma's speech; on each occasion he keeps the camera stationary but
reverses the angle, thus emphasizing confusion of identity. Alma
finally strives to return to herself: 'I don't feel like you, I don't

think like you, I'm not you ... I'm Sister Alma ... I would very much like to have – I love – I haven't – ' (p. 97). Language offers no solution. She tries once more to break Elisabet's silence but only draws a reluctant 'nothing' ('ingenting'). No-thing is reliable; as Alma puts it: '. . . and then all the many words. I, me, we, us, no, what is it, where is closest, where can I get a grip?' (p. 93).

In the film, language mainly exists as monologue, radio/television speech, and printed word. All these forms indicate potential traps. This corresponds to Bergman's long-standing suspicion of language which is, he tells Charles Thomas Samuels, 'a very ... bad channel between writer and performer' (*Essays in Criticism*, p. 112), admitting that 'it has always been difficult for me to find the word I want' (p. 101). Alma's powers of articulation falter; at one point, like Beckett's Lucky, she talks nonsense. Bergman says that Alma's aggressions 'take on such enormous proportions she finds she can no longer use words' (*Bergman on Bergman*, p. 203). Her babble complements cinematic 'nonsense' in certain dislocated or accelerated sequences. By means of split frames, uncoordinated shots, soft-focus and a blank screen, Bergman proves that if human speech can collapse via nonsense into silence, then so can the language of film. Alma's trauma discloses a void, the 'nothing' beyond which Elisabet will not vocally commit herself. Nor does Bergman commit himself further. The film ends with Alma, calm and collected, taking a bus back to town. Her mental state is open to conjecture; yet perhaps its balance, which permits social integration and compromise, has been so upset, that only now can she re-establish some kind of harmony between her inner self and outward action.

This tension bears directly upon the place of artists in society. In *Persona*, a combination of this theme with formal unrest implies that Bergman is questioning his own artistic integrity. Elisabet Vogler is a successful actress, but on forgetting her lines she feels a tremendous desire to laugh, seemingly at the absurdity of her own situation. The next day, her housekeeper finds her mute and immobile. She remains like this for three months, then Alma takes charge of her. One day, in Elisabet's hospital bedroom, the two women hear a soap opera on the radio. An actress declaims:

'Forgive me ... darling ... so that I can ... live again' (p. 29). Elisabet turns up the volume, breaks into laughter, then brusquely switches off the radio. She refuses to tolerate such blatant mockery of genuine emotion. For her, these sentimental effusions are evidence of the artist as charlatan (a central theme in *The Face*). Unaware that Elisabet now scorns art, Alma talks of its 'colossal' importance, then hastily apologises: 'I don't think I'd better talk about these things when you're listening, Mrs Vogler. I'll be getting into deep waters' (p. 31). Yet music still moves Elisabet: like Ester in *The Silence*, she listens peacefully to it on the radio.

If language is inane and speech is ineffective, then acting is pointless and even irresponsible in view of harsh reality. Elisabet elects to be silent, like the Old Man in *The Ghost Sonata*: 'I prefer silence — then one can hear thoughts and see the past. Silence cannot hide anything — but words can'. In the hospital, Elisabet hears 'meaningless words, fragments of sentences; syllables, mixed together or dropping at even intervals' (p. 32). This collage of vague sounds, developed later in *Cries and Whispers*, seems as inept to Elisabet as were her own words in the theatre. *Through a Glass Darkly* initiates this suspicion of language (David battles with 'winding sentences' and 'hateful words'); it grows in *The Silence*, and erupts in *Persona* which, says Susan Sontag, 'demonstrates ... the lack of an appropriate language, a language that's genuinely full' (*Styles of Radical Will*, p. 144). Elisabet reacts dramatically to a discrepancy between her stylized language and that of daily life.

Elisabet's shock on seeing a television newsreel of a Vietnamese suicide is partly her overwrought conscience registering a gap between theatrical dilettantism and the violent world at large, partly a response to the immediacy of the medium. Bergman does not believe that fictional creations can compete against the instantaneity of television. Its dramatic authenticity makes it more difficult for an artist to justify his function in a community, especially if, like Bergman, he avoids ideological commitment. Redundancy threatens the artist, who necessarily feeds off the raw material of life. Elisabet's job distances her from the world, which the mass-media so vividly represent. Her conscience obliges her to renounce her impotent work; it also tells her that refuge in silence is a cowardly half measure, in comparison with the finality of the Vietnamese monk's self-immolation. Yet the morality of her behaviour is clearly and intentionally an open question. Bergman says 'the silence that she cultivates is non-neurotic. It is a strong person's way of protesting' (*Bergman on Bergman*, p. 211). It is, therefore, positive action, a symbolic suicide, particularly as it rules out any possibility of Elisabet continuing her career. It lures Alma into self-revealing statements; Raymond Durgnat – giving Warhol's soup cans as one example – maintains that such provocative passivity is fundamental to so-called 'meaningless' art.

The psychiatrist confronts Elisabet with an explanation of the silence. According to this, although Elisabet realizes the duality of her existence – 'the abyss between what you are for others and what you are for yourself' (p. 41) – she simply assumes a new role: illness. As Ester says in *The Silence*, 'We try them out, one attitude after another, and find them all meaningless' (*A Film Trilogy*, p. 140). Elisabet's introspection turns out as unsatisfactory as her former exposure: 'Your hiding place isn't watertight enough. Life starts leaking in everywhere. And you're forced to react' (p. 41). In 'The Snake's Skin' – an essay written for Bergman's acceptance of the Erasmus Prize in 1965, and published in the script of *Persona* – he recalls his own retreat from life and art. Alma's inquisitiveness about Elisabet mirrors Bergman's own 'insatiable curiosity', which propels him into creativity, sociability and identity within the community. Bergman likens this ambivalent back and forth movement to a contrast of long shot and close-up in his cinematic style. The unsealed letter, which Alma secretly reads, represents the toxic potential of written language. Thinking that chatter is more natural, Alma criticizes Elisabet's silence as a selfish way of taking a break from her roles. Ironically, Alma does not believe that Elisabet is being herself, yet it is Alma who is heading for Elisabet's denuded state.

In the course of a rather smug summary, which the film omits in the interests of an open ending, the psychiatrist (symbolizing reason, health and sanity) nonetheless makes a crucial remark: 'Personally I would say that you have to be fairly infantile to cope with being an artist in an age like ours' (p. 99). This hinges on the redundancy idea, and Bergman's admission that 'artists are hardly the social visionaries they used to be' (*Bergman on Bergman*, p. 210). He refers this problem back to a dissociation of art and worship in the Renaissance apotheosis of individualism. Hence the divine silence of the trilogy. Bergman says: 'The artist considers his isolation, his subjectivity, his individualism almost holy' (*Four Screenplays*, xxii). The pretentious vanity of this holiness stuns Elisabet, so she embarks on a nihilistic but honest silence. Knowing that society preserves art, so will not coerce her, she forces herself into decisive activity, or, rather, passivity. Mistakenly rejecting motherhood, she switches to a posture in which, hopefully for her, roles do not apply.

Persona is an orchestration rather than a narration, inviting the spectator to challenge his own preconceptions. Bergman's chosen medium (film) reflects his feelings about another (language), while showing its own peculiar vulnerability in the medial breakdown. This sequence, one of three in which Bergman stresses the mechanical nature of film, consists of a medley of sound (machine-gun, dissonant music, cries, gibberish) in support of incoherent images (split frame, slapstick, eye, nail through hand, blurred shot of Elisabet parting curtains and walking about). In the television sequence, Bergman utilizes what Kracauer calls 'asynchronous sound' (a technique also employed by Godard) to stress the fraudulence of language; image (the public suicide) does not correspond to sound (report of a military clash). Balázs maintains that:

> Silence ... is an acoustic effect, but only where sounds can be heard. The presentation of silence is one of the most specific dramatic effects of the sound film. No other art can reproduce silence, neither painting nor sculpture, neither literature nor the silent film could do so (p. 205).

As in the trilogy, Bergman relies almost exclusively on natural sound, strikingly evident in certain sequences notable for their dramatic use of silence. Three such sequences are:

(i) when Alma stops the car by a lake, to read the unsealed letter.

We hear only the distinctive sound of raindrops.

(ii) when Elisabet enters Alma's room at night. The only sounds are raindrops and ship horns out at sea. Their contrasting repetition (short-long, high-low) contributes to the eeriness of the scene.

(iii) when Alma refrains from clearing up the broken glass. Her expression (and the camera angle) suffice to convey the meaning of the incident.

Bergman specializes in facial close-up; as Balázs says: 'The physiognomy of men is more intense when they are silent. More than that, in silence even things drop their masks' (p. 207). Throughout this film, sound creates dramatic tension, corroborating Balázs' view that 'the experience of silence is essentially a space experience. We feel the silence when we can hear the most distant sound or the slightest rustle near us' (p. 206). For example, in the scene where Elisabet sends Alma off with letters, an ominous atmosphere is generated solely by the sound of a slamming door, creaking chairs, pouring rain and heavy breathing. Bergman eschews conventional film music, allowing sound to take its place. In *Persona* music is scarce and exclusively atonal; at crucial points, it rises to a discordant crescendo, merging on one occasion with a roll of thunder.

Bergman refuses to offer a consistent narrative. He applies a principle of the 'New Novel' to film, placing *Persona* beside similar post-modern milestones, like Fellini's $8\frac{1}{2}$ and Resnais' *Last Year at Marienbad*, which attest to the worth of extensive ambiguity and uncertain denouement. Bergman says: 'Today, when I see how badly the novel has gone off the rails and how less and less able we are to experience and accept a fictitious course of events in an elemental way, the more reluctant I have become to tell stories with a beginning and an end' (*Bergman on Bergman*, p. 210). Singular interpretation becomes as vulnerable as language or the reel of film. Bergman settles for a two-way arrangement; in a preface to the script, he invites the imagination of reader/spectator to 'dispose freely' of the material at his disposal. Bergman thus takes pains to free his work from prescriptive delusions of language and art.

Shame

Shame — in Robin Wood's view 'one of the very few films of recent years that really matter' — is shot in black and white, and the stark mezzotints suit the subject exactly. The moral of the film has been stated very clearly by Bergman himself: 'We've disinherited ourselves. We're on the slippery slope. There's no stopping developments — things have gone too far already. The opposing forces are too few, too badly organized, too nonplussed, too helpless. What's going on in the West is all to hell. And we know it. And it's getting worse' (*Bergman on Bergman*, p. 232). This is quite unambiguous, making for a movie that is unclouded by the usual Bergman preoccupation with God and the Devil. This is a political film, about how ordinary men and women behave in situations of anarchy and great stress.

The protagonists, Eva and Jan, are living on an island in Sweden. Formerly violinists in an orchestra, they now run a smallholding. A civil war is raging in the rest of the country, but this has not yet impinged on the lives of the island's inhabitants. As the film opens Jan and Eva come up against the first signs — early ominous notes — that the conflict is beginning to encroach on their sheltered world: the telephone rings, but no one is at the end of the line; and church bells ring on a Friday. They get up early in order to deliver trays of soft fruit to the mayor. In the town, they see transport vehicles of various kinds and heavily equipped soldiers in the streets. Groups of people — possibly refugees — stand about with their bundles and cases, and the loudspeaker system broadcasts messages which the couple do not understand. Their radio at home has not been working properly for quite some time, and this trip to the town forces them into a realization that things are rapidly getting serious. It appears from something they are told that a landing is imminent. They visit an old friend, an antique dealer, who has just been called up; the strange timelessness of this scene is stressed by shots of ornaments from a bygone age. The dealer is afraid of the prospect, and shares a bottle of wine with them in a state of some tension. 'No one knows why it still goes on', he says. 'Yesterday, our radio threatened the most awful things. This morning their radio answered, congratulating us on our imminent destruction. It's all utterly incomprehensible' (*Persona and Shame*, p. 120). The mayor, too, seems worried. But, for the present at least, Jan and Eva Rosenberg are not themselves in any danger. There now occurs the sunniest and happiest sequence in the entire film, and it is placed at this strategic point in order that all subsequent sequences should appear in progressively greater contrast to this brief moment of happiness. This is how Bergman outlines it in his working draft:

> They come home in the afternoon. Sit in the sun by the wall of the house and eat boiled salmon-trout and drink white wine. For once the table is laid, with some autumn flowers in a cream jug. The dachshund is under Eva's chair. The cat is on the steps. The summery buzzing of a bee.
>
> (p. 122)

In the conversation which follows Eva shows that she is deeply disappointed their marriage so far has remained childless, and nags Jan about his lack of practical know-how in fixing the waste-pipe in the kitchen and doing other necessary jobs about the house. Suddenly, however, her mood becomes softer and he tells her she is beautiful in the soft light and she answers him that they've had a good day. Their hands meet and they sink to the ground in each other's arms.

The light has changed when the next sequence opens: it is already evening, and more sombre and ominous. An air-battle takes place over their heads, and a fighter aircraft crashes dramatically near their house. Jan sees the tortured body of the pilot who has bailed out dangling from a tree. Immediately afterwards they are advised by soldiers on their own side to flee the area as quickly as possible. It is dusk when they start packing and almost dark as they leave. They are prevented from going by enemy paratroopers leaping at them from the darkness and forcing them to give a television interview later to be faked and broadcast for propaganda purposes by the enemy station. A burst of firing puts an end to this, and the enemy vanish as swiftly as they had come. Exhausted and upset by their ordeal, Jan and Eva give up the idea of leaving immediately and go straight to bed. As they lie together trying to keep each other warm, Eva says how glad she is that they haven't had any children. 'For them', comments Bergman, 'this is the first day of the war' (p. 135).

At dawn they are awoken by shattering explosions and feel that 'the world is coming to an end' (p. 135). Confused and disorientated they try again and again to find a way out of the area. (As Robin Wood comments, 'journeys in the first half of the film are abortive attempts at flight, all of which end in a return to the house, and the journey at the end is a voyage to nowhere'). They pass a burning farm and see the bodies of the occupants who have been shot: there they also come across a dead child and a burnt-out tank – Liv Ullmann's shocked eyes in this sequence are the most haunting image of the entire movie. It seems that the enemy landing has been repulsed and indeed gradually the sound of firing dies down and Jan and Eva return home to an uneasy calm. A few days later they are picked up for questioning in connection with the falsified television interview they gave to the enemy soldiers. They are roughed about somewhat, but do not come to any serious harm. The mayor, a man called Jacobi, picks them out from the crowd of collaborators and takes them into his office for a friendly word. He then sends them home in his own car.

A few weeks later a cease-fire is signed and the autumn sets in; Jan and Eva are trying to plant potatoes, but they are starting to quarrel more and more viciously. The constant terror of death and brutality is undermining even their common decency and affection for each other. It is clear that Jacobi has been helping a lot by keeping them supplied both with items in short supply such as paraffin, and with luxury goods like radios, brandy and even jewellery. Jacobi, who has sent his wife away to Switzerland, is obviously a lonely man, and more and more frequently seeks out their company. Jan is vaguely aware that this is compromising them. His fear is confirmed when Jacobi comes round one day and stays much longer than usual. While Jan is befuddled with drink, Jacobi and Eva make love in the greenhouse. Before, Jacobi has given Eva a large sum of money, saying she is his 'heir'. Perhaps he does this to pay her for sleeping with him, perhaps just for safe-keeping. Whatever the truth, the partisans emerge from the woods and seize Jacobi. They offer a deal: since their organization is in need of ready cash, they will free Jacobi if he pays them a substantial sum of money. Jan, who knows of the money and who took it when he realized Eva had gone to the greenhouse with Jacobi, pretends he does not know what they are talking about. The Resistance fighters smash up the house and set it on fire, and then force Jan to shoot Jacobi with a revolver.

The final section of the film opens with Jan and Eva camping out in the greenhouse. They hardly talk to each other now; Eva weeps violently from time to time, and Jan strikes her more and more frequently. A young deserter from their own side takes refuge with them, and Jan, to Eva's horror, shoots him in order to take over his boots and equipment. Before he kills the young man, he finds out from him that a boat is leaving the next day at dawn, and that for a consideration they might be able to get on board. They put their few belongings together and trek to the coast. They find that the boat is run by the Resistance leader who had ordered Jan to shoot Jacobi (and the same man who had sold them salmon-trout earlier in the film). By paying over Jacobi's money, Jan and Eva are allowed to take their place in the open boat, which pushes off out to sea. Days follow as their supplies run out and more and more people in the boat die. The boat drifts among floating corpses which Bergman says are a reminiscence of a grim photograph in *Life* magazine: 'During the last war, or just after it, they'd photographed a torpedoed troop transport. They'd found masses of dead people floating about in the Atlantic. It all looks thoroughly stylized . . . It's all so unreal it seems to have been staged' (*Bergman on Bergman*, p. 233). It is with this terrifyingly real and at the same time surreal image of shapeless bodies floating in the sea around the doomed open boat on a dreary and menacingly calm sea that Bergman ends this the starkest of all his films.

It is a movie which invites comparison with *The Seventh Seal* in more ways than one: the skyline shot near the end, for instance. There is the obvious fact, too, about the apocalyptic nature of both films, although *The Seventh Seal* is set in medieval Sweden and *Shame* in a contemporary or even slightly futuristic world. But there is also the magic number seven in the title of the earlier movie, and the fact that *Shame* is divided into seven major sections. The first section is introductory and shows Jan and Eva getting up and leaving for the town with their lingonberries; the second shows them on the drive to the town during which they buy fish from the man called Philip, and a bottle of wine from their antique-dealer friend. The third is the happiness of the meal and the destruction of their happiness with the arrival of the military from both sides. The fourth section deals with the battle, and the fifth the interrogation. The sixth tells of Eva's infidelity, the first such lapse which — we are told — has occurred during their marriage; and the seventh and last section finds them on the desolate sea. The couple have exhausted their relationship to the bitter dregs whilst at the same time the world itself has disintegrated finally around them. There is nothing to hope for and death seems certain.

Shame is considered by some reviewers as going too far in its pessimism. Yet the film is not unrealistically gloomy. It is filmed in a documentary style with very rapid, even jerky camera movements, and with heavy emphasis on grey light. There is no accompanying music although music is mentioned two or three times with great nostalgia by the protagonists. The film thus offers itself as an unemotional account of the way society and individuals break up in conditions of extreme stress. Other film makers have confirmed this in interesting ways; for instance, Louis Malle's *Lacombe, Lucien* is an equally unsentimental portrait of conditions of civil strife and collaboration, in this case set in France in the early 1940's. Although Malle's film is in colour, the emotions and the message are almost as stark and uncompromising as Bergman's: that most people behave with cringing pusillanimity in moments of crisis, especially when they are deprived of all the normal standards and material goods to which they are accustomed. Bergman explains that his inspiration was not indeed very far from Malle's:

The Shame originates in a panicky question: how would I

Stills from *Shame*

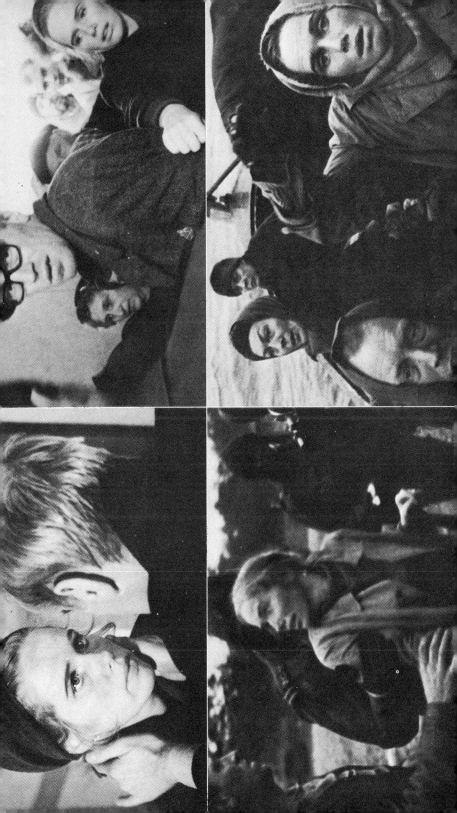

have behaved during the Nazi period if Sweden had
been occupied and if I'd held some position of responsibility or been connected with some institution? Or had
even found myself threatened as a private person? How
much civic courage would I have been able to muster up
under the threat of violence, physical or spiritual, or in
the war of nerves in an occupied country? Every time
I've thought about such matters, I've always come to
the same conclusion: physically and psychically I'm a
coward . . . The long, cold, wearing threat – how would
I survive that? (*Bergman on Bergman*, p. 228).

The simplicity of the narrative and the grainy style of the photography thus perfectly suit the 'it happened here' nature of the story.
It is quite legitimate for Bergman to ask how the peace-loving
neutral Swedes would behave if they found their country torn apart
by civil war. The answer is, certainly no better, and possibly worse
than other people; for instance a lot worse than the Vietnamese,
whose troubles partly inspired Bergman when he was thinking
about making *Shame* (in fact it is a kind of re-enactment of the
Vietnamese civil war in a Swedish context – the same ideological
conflict barely understood by its principal victims). Everyone in
the movie is shown up as being pusillanimous to some degree:
Philip the resistance leader, Jacobi the mayor (who is described by
Eva as 'just a scared little man doing a dirty job that no one else
would take', p. 185), and of course Jan Rosenberg himself. Only
Eva emerges from the story with anything approaching dignity.

Eric Rhode entitled his review in *The Listener* 'Everyman's Land',
thereby indicating the universal application of this story. It is a
story which begins in late summer and ends in the depth of winter,
and the declining curve, from the light effects we associate with
Smiles of a Summer Night to those we are presented with in *Winter
Light*, is characteristic not only of this film but also of the
dramaturgical curve we find in all of Bergman's movies. Moreover
it is no accident that Jan dreams of a time when he and Eva were
rehearsing under Dorati the fourth Brandenburg concerto, and in
particular the slow movement. This particular piece of music, an

andante in 3/4 time, is a movement in which the flutes and violins answer each other in alternation, and has been described as a 'beautiful and grave piece, in mournful measure'. The description applies equally well to *Shame*, thoughout which the muted instruments of Eva and Jan answer each other in progressively more mournful measure.

The title, *Shame*, is perfectly apposite to the theme. Bergman is quite frank about the fact that as a Swede living in a highly-developed and peaceful country he is protected from many of the horrors which other people have known all too often in this century. This explains why *Persona* is articulated around the scene on television where a Buddhist monk burns himself to death in the street in Saigon in protest against governmental religious policy, and around the photograph of the little boy being rounded up with other Jews by German soldiers in the Warsaw ghetto. Jan and Eva's direct confrontation with the experiences of war — like Elisabet Vogler's reaction to its images — endorses Robin Wood's affirmation that the artist can 'no longer ... shut his consciousness off from the fact of needless and appalling suffering' (p. 143). Such cruelties, remote from the Swedish experience, inevitably provoke 'shame' in the author, and he is concerned to pass it on to the spectator. Bergman is, in fact, adept at imposing his own sense of shame on those who watch his films; it is impossible not to feel involved by the thrust that he makes. This film is about infamy, degradation, and the sinister banality of cruelty and suffering. As such, the episode where Eva in the middle of the film sits up and says, 'Sometimes everything seems like a long strange dream. It's not my dream, it's someone else's, that I'm forced to take part in' (p. 145) is, he claims, his 'aesthetic and ethical figleaf' (*Bergman on Bergman*, p. 235). This is because she believes that when the person who has dreamt the dream in which she figures wakes up, he or she will be 'ashamed' of the dream.

That declaration addressed straight from the middle of the film to the spectator is an expression of Bergman's 'moral embarrassment'. He is at once apologizing for the bad dream he is imposing upon the spectator, and forcing him to dream the dream because it is true. Eva accuses *us* of the fact that she has not borne a child, and yet if she had had a baby it would have suffered a horrible fate. When she dreams, at the very end of the film, that she holds her baby in her arms, we realize the extent of her loss: but at the same time we recognize that in the circumstances it is far better she has never had any children at all. This relief at sterility in a sterile landscape is the kind of sombre message which Bergman gives us in a manner very similar to Beckett. Like Beckett, he shows that words lose their meaning, as Jan and Eva talk less and less to each other and sink into longer and longer periods of silence. Like Beckett, too, he offers a portrait of the artist as someone 'on an equal footing with every other creature who also exists solely for his own sake . . . in selfish fellowship on the warm, dirty earth, under a cold and empty sky' (p. 15). This is probed cruelly by Jacobi:

> JACOBI: This business of being an artist. Is it all it's cracked up to be? Does it free you from all your obligations? You're wrong. It's no longer possible to refer everyone simply to the colossal sensitivity of your soul. Say what you like, do what you like, okay. But take the risks. You don't want me here. I understand. So you've told me.
>
> EVA: Don't be stupid. You're drunk and you're talking nonsense.
>
> JACOBI: I saw you just got frightened. If I sniff at your arm-pits now they'll smell of fear. It's a pity I like you. That you've come to be my friends in the twilight of the world. Otherwise I'd send you to a labour camp. Are you afraid, Jan Rosenberg? Are you an artist or a sack?
>
> JAN: I'm a sack. But sit down and let's talk about something else. We could listen to a little music, for instance.
>
> JACOBI: The holy freedom of art, the holy gutlessness of art. I will pay no attention to Eva's remarkable contribution to the conversation. Now let's listen. (Sings). I'm going out for a piss.
>
> (pp. 163-4)

Bergman's 'portrait of the artist' is very harsh; but we are never allowed to forget that it is in large measure a self-portrait. He invites us to share his shame, his shame at being alive and sometimes happy in a terrible and ever worsening world.

A Passion

> *What is this deadly poison that*
> *never ceases to corrode the best in us,*
> *leaving only the shell?* (Eva)

A Passion crystallizes Bergman's study of isolated individuals, confirming their failure to live with others and their inevitable exposure to private and public suffering. He gives unconditional priority to a theme about which he formerly had mixed feelings: '... the individual has become the highest form and the greatest bane of artistic creation. The smallest wound or pain of the ego is examined under a microscope as if it were of eternal importance' (*Four Screenplays*, pp. 21-2). The film derives peculiar force from a sustained conflict of opposites — for instance, between withdrawal and involvement. Andreas Winkelman feels this tension when, after a spell in prison and the break-up of his marriage, he leaves his former friends and scientific work to live alone for a long time on a lonely island. He foolishly believes that his new life bears no relation to his past, discovering instead that his solitude and independence are as perturbing as they are desirable. His refuge appears to liberate but in fact immures him. The more he tries to cut himself off, the more he hankers after contact and companionship. He falls between two stools, aware that withdrawal is a snare and delusion, yet fearing that involvement will invite the kind of failure in life which originally precipitated his retreat. His frustration recalls David's remark in *Through a Glass Darkly* about protecting 'our private game' with a 'magic circle,' only to find out that 'every time life smashes the circle the game turns into something grey, tiny, ridiculous. So one draws a new circle, builds up new barriers' (*A Film Trilogy*, p. 54). This also invites comparison

with Strindberg's *The Dance of Death*, where interpersonal hell
holds sway on an island fortress, causing Kurt, the Quarantine
Officer, to declare: 'My position will bring me into contact with
everyone. And it won't be plain sailing, because however little
one wants to, one's bound to become involved in other people's
intrigues.'

Andreas defends his independence but admits later that 'freedom is a frightful gift', if only because it is no automatic passport
to lasting felicity. His happiness, measurable only in selfish terms,
is sporadic and short-lived. The long-term inadequacy of his
yardstick is proved by the fact that no matter how he resists, people
and events intrude on his privacy and colour his behaviour. Like
Pastor Tomas, Andreas learns that 'we live our simple daily lives.
And then some terrible piece of information forces itself into our
secure, safe world. It's more than we can bear' (*A Film Trilogy*,
p. 74). Unpredictability is a disturbing feature of this unavoidable
involvement. Andreas meets Anna Fromm quite by chance: one
day she shows up at his house to use the telephone. The critic,
Vernon Young maintains that her dead husband (also Andreas) and
Winkelman are one and the same person, the film basically re-
enacting previous hostilities. Young proceeds to interpret the film
as a Christian allegory (the film's American title is *The Passion of
Anna*) but in spite of Anna's religious attitude − 'I didn't believe
that life could be a daily martyrdom' − the 'passion' might equally
be that of Andreas, his neighbour Eva, or the old woodman, Johan
Andersson. The suffering inherent in Christ's passion afflicts every
character in the film, rendering Young's reading somewhat forced,
as is his double-Andreas contention, although the dialogue at
times suggests it. It is unnecessary, anyway, to interpret the film
according to such a complex sense of *déjà vu*; the point is not so
much whether the two Andreases are in fact identical but rather
that so many of Bergman's people fit a common description and
suffer from the same personal 'disease.'

Anna's arrival signals the beginning of their affair, steeped
throughout in guile and concealment. Andreas pretends to close
the door on her telephone conversation and lurks inside to overhear
her distraught remarks; having gleaned enough, he exits quietly.

Bergman uses the door as a dramatic device, as in the schoolhouse scene in *Winter Light*, or in *The Touch*, when Karin leaves David in his apartment. In *A Passion*, the door itself is a reconstruction of the stained-glass door that profoundly struck Bergman during his childhood visits to Uppsala; here its artificial reflection helps to establish a mood of superficial warmth and deception. A ticking clock is the only accompaniment to this tense scene. When Anna finishes her call, Andreas almost inevitably invites her to use the telephone whenever she likes, just as he cannot later resist contact with Eva on finding her asleep in her car. Anna forgets her handbag, resulting in Andreas rummaging through it and reading a letter to her from her husband that forecast 'physical and psychical acts of violence.' There are several subsequent flashbacks to this revealing phrase.

The couple later attempt to coexist in blissful ignorance of the darker side of their personalities. We learn that Andreas has forged cheques, driven while drunk and hit a policeman. Like Jan and Eva in *Shame*, or Johan Borg in *Hour of the Wolf*, we see in Andreas and Anna intelligent, creative individuals whose output has all but ceased. Once more, language is a barrier. Anna is a translator, Andreas a geologist. The house – stocked with books, in a typically Scandinavian 'natural' interior, beautifully shot by Nykvist – is conducive to undisturbed study but both seem paralyzed by their own complexes, unable to communicate their real feelings and ideas in the written or spoken word (in the outhouse a potting wheel also lies idle). The only work that Andreas undertakes is the rather uninspiring task of scribe for Eva's husband, his architect neighbour, Elis Vergerus; but even then he does it less out of intellectual commitment than financial exigency.

Anna's naive religious candour cuts little ice with Andreas, whose own lack of scruple in reading private letters brings him some knowledge of Anna's potential for mental cruelty. During the fateful letter-reading sequence, Bergman rivets his audience not only by the prominent tick of the clock (as if echoing the tap of the typewriter keys) but also by shooting the written words in uncompromising close-up. It transpires that Anna's husband was on the verge of leaving her when he and their son were killed in an accident while Anna was driving. She still bears the mark of her own serious injury.

Anna expects everyone to comply with her own rigorous moral fervour. She cannot accept others' weaknesses. At dinner in the Vergerus' house, she criticizes their cynicism, bragging about her self-esteem and forthright marriage, which we know to be a lie: 'I try to busy myself with things I believe in . . .' In many ways, Anna is more frightening than Andreas in her self-deceit; she reflects Bergman's consciousness of his own moralistic, puritanical side.

Andreas pretends that his philosophy of spiritual scepticism and rustic simplicity can compensate fully for his diffidence, lack of self-control and fear of freedom. Yet, like the Captain in *The Dance of Death*, he is driven to accept that 'there comes a moment when the ability to create in imagination . . . fails. And then reality stands out in all its nakedness.' In one scene, Andreas stumbles drunkenly through the woods calling out his own name, as if in doubt of his identity. In his stupor he is both clinging to a vanishing ideal and demonstrating his insignificance. The scene is desolate and wintry; distant foghorns boom a warning. Bergman stresses Andreas's lack of importance by shooting this sequence mainly in a tracking shot from a high angle. This emphasis on non-entity befits Bergman's attitude towards Fårö, but the difference between his own island life and that of his tortured character is that Bergman has been there mainly in the evenings or at weekends, relaxing from the fray of a hectic professional commitment to stage or studio, whereas Andreas tries to lose himself totally in the seclusion of the island, with the result that its natural intransigence and stability start to oppress him.

Andreas declines to admit his faults to Anna but they show in his prying and later in his undisguised violence towards her. She counters with her own brand of violence, making as if to strangle Andreas during a love scene. Their relationship is a weird mixture of love and hate. His longing for partnership satisfied, Andreas perversely does his best to evade commitment. The result is an uneasy compromise. Another contradiction within Andreas is his kindness and thoughtlessness. He fits Elis's description of Anna's husband as a mixture of good nature and ruthlessness. With the injured puppy, the first victim of a maniacal animal torturer at large in the district, as with Eva and, later, a wounded bird, Andreas displays a compassion that is quite lacking in his dealings with Anna. Moreover, his sympathy with Johan, when the wood-man becomes the suspected perpetrator, does not extend to offer-ing shelter when Johan wonders where he can go to escape persecu-tion. Andreas is not just unwilling but also pathetically helpless in a way that equally affects the self-righteous Anna. When Johan helps the drunken Andreas, the latter is violent and abusive to him, yet at times Andreas shows genuine concern for the bronchial old man. The false accusation stirs Andreas's liberal indignation but he clearly does not know how to deal with the situation.

Andreas extends his involvement to Elis and Eva, with whom Anna initially stayed. Elis and Eva hide their incompatibility beneath a veil of bourgeois comfort. They typify the contrast between the privileged professionals on the island, whose affluence conveniently enables them to aestheticize the violence around them, and the peasant community, typified by Johan, who realizes his powerlessness in the face of cruelty and for whom the only escape is death. While Elis, owner of a large tract of land stretching down to the sea, gaily takes photographs in the cosy luxury of his windmill studio, to the accompaniment of baroque music and clinking whisky glasses, Johan commits suicide in his run-down cottage. Indeed, Elis accepts Johan as the suspect precisely *because* he is a recluse. Money, cynicism and scapegoating concur all too easily but, as Niels Jensen curtly observes, 'despair isn't rhetoric for Johan.'

Eva's gregarious façade cloaks a sexual and emotional emptiness – 'it's hard to realize one day that you're meaningless,' she tells Andreas. Elis wearily justifies his work by a commitment to her material needs; on the personal level he fails to satisfy her at all. Eva tells Andreas that she is merely a small part of his general ennui. Her insecurity renders her gullible and vulnerable – yet her casual affair with Andreas includes moments of genuine passion as well as evidence of his capacity for affection. Eva then lies on the phone to Elis, whose suspicious tone unnerves Andreas. Fearing Elis, Eva hastens to leave; in an extraordinary sequence after her departure,

Andreas nervously paces his house. In the distance, bells toll ominously. He lies down, suddenly emitting a desperate moan, like Karin in *Cries and Whispers*, or Nazerman (Rod Steiger) at a particularly painful moment in Lumet's *The Pawnbroker*. The suffering of these characters is so intense that words fail them; only primal noise can articulate their grief.

Elis is cool, calculating, cynical. An enthusiastic photographer, he is nonetheless sceptical of visual truth. He shows Andreas a picture of Eva, smiling and apparently happy; in fact, it was taken at the onset of a migraine. By using a character as mouthpiece – 'you look at the picture and give rein to your imagination.' – Bergman extends the doubts about the definitive visual image he entertained in *Persona*. Elis appears to be a model of respectable restraint but his ambiguous obsession with deceptive photography – mainly studies in violence and force – undermines this impression. The film thus consistently contrasts ideal with real experience. The inability of Andreas to reconcile the two gradually breaks him. He reflects Bergman's opinion that 'we walk in circles, so limited by our own anxieties that we can no longer distinguish between true and false, between the gangster's whim and the purest ideal' (*Four Screenplays*, p. 22). The actuality of evil and pain, added to his own misgivings, proves too much for the initial optimism of Andreas.

Bergman creates a pervasive atmosphere right from the start. The opening scene of the film brilliantly initiates the process of disillusionment. Over the credits we hear tinkling sheep bells and strange music; the bells take over as the establishing shot reveals a flock shifting ground; then we cut to a middle close-up of Andreas mending a roof, while Bergman narrates some information about his protagonist and the state of his roof. Already things start going wrong – a bucket tumbles from the roof, spilling cement. This incident, like life itself, is unpredictable and causes a mess; later, on finding the hanging puppy, Andreas drops his bucket and pine-cones spill out. The symbols are obvious but perfectly appropriate and unforced. Andreas looks up from his work to survey the idyllic scene, only to witness a brief optical illusion in which three suns appear in the sky. This dissolve is accompanied by the spine-chilling sounds of a gathering wind and distant dog barks; the landscape turns cold and threatening, portending troublous events. Such use of omens recalls *The Face*, while in *The Seventh Seal* we hear of horses devouring each other and a similar parhelion.

Meaningless violence soon spoils Andreas's dream. He and Anne indulge in a series of 'physical and psychical acts,' culminating in a vicious assault on Anna by Andreas, shot close-up with a hand held camera and with the noise of the wind as a harsh acoustic support. Their behaviour corresponds to that of the person who sets fire to horses, hangs dogs and mutilates sheep. These perversions lead to the beating up of Johan by irate islanders who wrongly accuse him of the crimes. When Johan kills himself, after being forced into a humiliating confession, Andreas has to read his dead friend's letter to the police. The abuse of Johan is described vividly in the letter, according with Bergman's belief that 'the story ... must have a suggestive effect on you, enable you to experience it deep down inside you, in your own cinematograph – much more drastically, brutally, honestly ... than I could ever show' (*Bergman on Bergman*, p. 209). Whether or not he likes it, Andreas cannot avoid implication. Johan's death highlights the collapse of communal trust and, by rejecting contact with others, Andreas contributes to the growth of the malaise that kills his friend. Andreas knew that Johan's life was in danger but underestimated or tried to ignore the fact. He and Anna can scrap with each other or calmly watch the televised execution of a Vietnamese prisoner, yet still believe that worldly violence is at a safe distance.

It takes Johan's death to force Andreas to recognize the harsh reality of the environment and the futility of his quasi-independent stance. He sees that silence is the sole defence against persecution and incrimination. Language spells involvement. One day, as he and Anna sit at their work-tables trying to get something done, he explains his feelings:

> Have you considered one thing? ... That the worse off people are, the less they complain. In the end they're totally silent. In spite of the fact that they are living

creatures with nerves and eyes and hands. Huge armies of victims and executioners. Light rising and falling heavily. Cold coming. Darkness. Heat. Smell. Everything is silent.

He maintains that they are trapped, a condition symbolized by the shot of a butterfly flapping on a window pane. He admits that he lives without self-respect and in fear of humiliation. He fantasizes about a past sexual encounter, possibly with his wife, in which she tells him he has 'cancer of the soul.' When Anna jolts him out of the daydream, he says he has been thinking about cancer – 'and it terrifies me.' His distraction recalls Persson in *Winter Light*, with his terror of the Chinese and the atomic bomb, except that Andreas must bear much of the guilt for his 'disease'.

Anna has a nightmare in which she repeatedly but vainly asks others for help. The sequence is composed of spare footage from *Shame*, in which Eva has a similar dream. Bergman originally intended *A Passion* to develop the war situation of the previous film in a more surreptitious, localized context. Eventually he played down the continuity yet both films retain a great deal in common. The nightmare, occurring significantly at Eastertide, contains a desperate, unavailing cry for forgiveness from Anna, anticipating Andreas's final refusal of forgiveness. On waking, Anna is aware only of shame, reiterating the theme of the previous film. The dream symbolism is complex but, on an immediately accessible level, we may see the dream as a desire for purgation. In both films, the women pass roaring fires; in *Shame*, roses are burning. We think of Eliot's lines in 'East Coker':

> If to be warmed, then I must freeze
> And quake in frigid purgatorial fires
> Of which the flame is roses, and the smoke is briars.

The sequence gains in force when Bergman cuts the soundtrack as Anna enters a ruined village; her panic is expressed in her soundless screams and, as in *Wild Strawberries*, by drumbeats and a ticking watch. Bergman again chooses to eschew music in favour of alternating silence and natural sound; the only music in the film comes from records in Elis's windmill and at Andreas's house.

Anna nearly has another car crash, Bergman creating suspense by the use of premonitory timpani strokes. As the car jerks to a halt, we see a hanging bear-charm swing around. Andreas gets out in pouring rain. He is at his wits' end, a 'whipped cur', like the puppy he rescued, of which the swinging charm reminds us. Anna drives off, leaving him in desolate marshland by a gnarled tree and a telegraph pole. This final scene recapitulates the unbearable tension in Andreas between resolution and vacillation, illusion and truth. The final shot completes the picture of his disintegration. Robin Wood refers to a similar shot of Johan Borg in *Hour of the Wolf*, at a critical moment in the castle, when the camera tracks right up to his face until the image dissolves. A slow zoom-in reduces Andreas to little more than an indistinct mass, as we hear a familiar tick from the letter sequence. The shot observes him pacing back and forth like a caged lion. Finally he lies down. Snow is falling. Feeble and forlorn, stuck in the middle of nowhere, Andreas brings to mind the description of Faust by Care, towards the end of Goethe's tragedy:

> Shall he go? Shall he come? He can't make up his mind.
> In the middle of the trodden road he totters and he
> fumbles, seeing more and more awry, getting more and
> more confused; a burden to himself, a burden to others
> ... thwarted, driven ... All this fixes him where he is
> and prepares him for hell.
>
> (tr. Barker Fairley)

The ultimate irony is that, unlike Faust or the lion, Andreas still has free will. He remains unable to accept at face value himself and those around him. Like the Captain in *The Dance of Death*, he cannot understand why life is so 'strange' and 'vindictive' and he becomes vindictive too. Like George in Polanski's *Cul-de-Sac*, who hunches bemused on a rock as the sea closes in, Andreas — his world collapsed around him — disappears in the middle of the grainy image. As at the end of *Shame*, where Jan and Eva drift to their death on the open sea, Andreas is left suspended in an existence

barely worth prolonging. Bergman's final words of narration –
'this time he was called Andreas Winkelman' – imply that he is not
only the second Andreas destroyed partly by Anna but also the
latest addition to Bergman's gallery of bedevilled beings.

Interviewed by the Swedish critic and filmmaker Stig Björkman, in *American Cinematographer* (April 1972), Bergman says:
'Film may be specially visual. For me, it goes on to develop itself in
rhythm and in light.' *A Passion* adheres to this formula, concentrating on a colour code of deep reds, browns and green, plus black and
white in Anna's dream. Light-dark contrasts are especially effective
in snowy conditions – one striking shot reveals, after Anna's fight
with Andreas, her red headscarf lying in the snow like a pool of
blood.

The film has an unusual rhythm – an episodic structure, frequently elliptical and interspersed with four interviews between
Bergman and his main actor/actresses. Bergman's strategic conception of these breaks is evident from his definition of each as a
'mellanspel' (literally, 'dramatic interlude'). It is curious that the
women, unlike the men, improvise their pieces. Max Von Sydow
refers to Andreas's hiding place as a 'prison', then Liv Ullmann says
that the trouble with 'believers' like Anna is that they unfairly
demand the same belief as others. Bibi Andersson expresses a wish
to see Eva 'blessed,' expecting her to achieve 'immense relief and a
feeling of peace' – Bergman finally bleaching her image to suggest
(as when sun lights up Johan's corpse, above which hangs a picture
of Christ haloed) martyrdom and a transfiguration. Last come
Erland Josephson's comments on Elis. These interpolations remind
us of Bergman's previous determination to show his audience that
Persona was, after all, a film; here they fulfil a similar function as
well as providing interesting insights into the principal characters.

A Passion shows that the way to truth and understanding cannot
exclude suffering which, in the words of another artist concerned
with isolation, Samuel Beckett, 'opens a window on the real and is
the main condition of the artistic experience' (*Proust*, p. 28). In a
Movie (no. 16) interview, Bergman says: 'I think films fulfil a
highly useful function in ritualizing violence. There people can
live it out and experience it. I believe the spectator achieves a kind

of liberation from watching these violent acts.' A controversial view, but one that draws a number of relevant parallels from mid-'sixties cinema onwards: for instance, Peckinpah's *Straw Dogs* and *The Wild Bunch*, Penn's *Bonnie and Clyde*, Boorman's *Deliverance*, Godard's *Weekend*, Friedkin's *The Exorcist* and Kubrick's *A Clockwork Orange*. Bergman's selectivity and stringent control of his material makes *A Passion* a highly responsible film, with a chillingly pertinent emphasis on the idea of latent virulence and barbarity in human nature.

The Touch

An anticlimax to the nihilistic intensity of *A Passion*, *The Touch* may at first disappoint us. It seems to offer little that is new to the follower of Bergman's isolation films. As before, Bergman places his characters in an affluent society perplexed by its personal and spiritual flaws. We meet another set of stressed individuals and get another instalment in Bergman's serial of weakness, violence and fear. Yet the film departs radically from its thematic stable-mates in Bergman's first use of the English language, an American actor (Elliott Gould) in a main part and a million-dollar budget from ABC Pictures Corporation. For Bergman, this was a 'marvellous' arrangement – in return for the Swedish made film, ABC gave him money and artistic control. Whatever the practical advantages of this partnership, we sense from the start a film of international box-office appeal that belies Bergman's impressive adherence to a purist approach. The plot is simple, occasionally trite; the film has a generally sleek audio-visual texture. Bergman intended to concentrate on Karin but was encouraged to develop the plot into a full-scale drama of passion. Gould's performance as Karin's lover is uneven, mainly because his part tends to invite gratuitous histrionics, whereas in the preceding films the integrality of single episodes – as shocking as they frequently are – is never in doubt.

Yet in spite of its apparent inconsistency, *The Touch* improves in retrospect, partly because it relieves the unremitting despair of its predecessors but also on account of forceful elements underlying its superficial banality. As we absorb the film, we see Bergman experimenting with a broader perspective on his recurrent themes.

The problem of isolation in this film relates to a bourgeois milieu in which, ironically, easy reach of other people and command of material comforts are the direct cause of individual discontent. This applies to Karin Vergerus (Bibi Andersson), thirty-four, wife of a hospital consultant in Visby on Gotland. The action centres on this island but in a predominantly urban setting, a far cry from the remote terrain that aggravates Winkelman's isolation in *A Passion*. Karin has a beautiful home and model family but her easy routine is stifling. She falls for David Kovac, a young American archaeologist on a dig at a local church. His volatile temperament appeals to the inwardly restless Karin. The film traces their turbulent affair and the destruction of Karin's domestic security. Although the plot establishes the eternal triangle, Bergman transcends the stereotypical situations by investigating their relationship as symptomatic of a malaise in contemporary Western life.

Bergman depicts the life of Karin and her husband Andreas as cushioned and regulated by their social status. We observe the effects of material superfluity (Karin cannot choose which one of numerous fashionable outfits to wear), the cloying comfort ('everything is almost painfully splendid', says Bergman) and the mechanical activity (Karin is a methodical housewife, Andreas has a rewarding job, they both tidy up automatically after guests have left). Andreas looks after his family but, like Fredrik in *Cries and Whispers*, puts his work before his wife's emotional and physical needs. As Karin increasingly stiffens to Andreas's tired advances, the distance grows between them, eroding their marital life. Bergman composes one middle long shot of the couple at opposite ends of the house – a fine setting in depth symbolizing their estrangement. Their children are healthy adolescents, although their daughter's 'first romance' with its exaggerated emotionalism ironically underscores her mother's equally nascent affair.

Karin is, in many ways, a typical Bergman woman, emotionally stronger and deeper than her male counterparts but trapped by her social and maternal role. David, on the other hand, is impulsive, energetic, unpredictable. Born in Germany, raised in the States, trained in Israel, based in London, he may remind us not only of a

tempestuous Lawrentian hero but also of Eliot's rootless Jew in
Gerontion, hybrid of several capitals. While the sharp contrast of
David's background and Karin's ethnic homogeneity at first seems
disruptive to the continuity of the film, we gradually see this
cultural clash underline the awkwardness of all forms of communication between the two.

Karin meets David's sister Sara on following him to London,
ignoring Andreas's calm but stern ultimatum: 'If you go you need
not come back'. Sara's congenital muscular complaint (evident in
David's own nervous instability and arthritic hands) intensifies the
exclusive bond between brother and sister. Bordering on a nervous
attack, Sara coldly informs Karin that she and David have 'everything in common.' This barrier drives Karin straight back to her
own kith and kin. She returns without seeing David. The confrontation between Sara and Karin takes place in a bare apartment in a
silent, hostile atmosphere. Bergman here displays his mastery of
cinematic pace – the sequence is agonizingly slow, in contrast to
the rapid montage of some earlier scenes.

David's struggle with his own personality manifests itself out-
wardly in selfishness, petulance and rage. When Andreas coolly
catches him making love to Karin, he reacts defiantly like a
mischievous child. We learn of David's attempted suicide, a fact
which 'gentle' Andreas does not hesitate to use as a psychological
weapon. Andreas's urbanity – like that of his 'relative' Elis in *A
Passion* – disguises a ruthless streak. Bergman spares few of his
characters.

David's insecurity also causes sexual problems ranging from
incontinence to impotence. This is a familiar Bergman complex,
recalling in particular *The Silence, Sawdust and Tinsel* and *Prison*.
One scene – David drunk, Karin confused – bears resemblance to
the garret scene in *Prison*, where Tomas drinks heavily in front of
the distressed Birgitta-Carolina. Both films also suggest a doomed
relationship – 'we're painfully united,' writes David. Karin wil-
lingly exposes herself to David's sexual roughness, whereby he
releases his inner frustration on her to save himself more hurt. He
upsets and frightens her but she cannot renounce him. The jealous
resentment, physical difficulties and ambivalent identities again

recall Strindberg, especially *Creditors* and *The Dance of Death*. In *The Dance of Death*, Alice returns uncertainly to the Captain; in *The Touch*, Karin finally decides to go back to Andreas, although pregnant by David and unsure of her husband's reception.

Karin returns more out of duty than genuine desire. This sense of duty plagues her affair – she can rationalize her former way of life but not her relationship with David, which simply 'happens', hence the importance of the 'touch.' Bergman repeatedly focuses on physical contact, yet we are always conscious of a block. David finds it hard to express himself in words, yet what should be unambiguous physical intimacy is equally fraught with doubt and fear. Even their most spontaneous expressions of mutual feeling seem tainted by the overwhelming influence of their respective backgrounds. David rejects Karin's ultimate decision as a lie. He insists that he loves her, maintaining that this fact both excuses his tantrums and precludes any compromises between them. Unable to accept either her prevarications or the conditions she puts on their meetings, he frequently loses his temper. Overestimating her ability to relinquish domestic commitments, he explodes on her arrival at his apartment inebriated from a business lunch. Yet he comes and goes as he pleases, while expecting her to drop everything when he is depressed and in need of her company. This capriciousness – so attractive to her at first – eventually adds to her unwillingness to follow him to an academic post in Denmark.

Karin's reversion to a familiar existence reflects Bergman's awareness of bourgeois repression, especially with regard to women. Karin's freedom to relate naturally to David is severely curtailed; their rendezvous are surreptitious breaks from household chores or social engagements. 'It is hard to live two lives' says Karin, and Bergman does not defend her choice, only shows the persuasive reasons for the 'miserable freedom' of Swedish society. Andreas is appropriately deferential and brutal; he tells Karin to make her decision and take the consequences – a fair remark, were it not for the deep rift he knows she feels between love for David and loyalty to her family. The final shot – of Karin alone in the park amongst fallen leaves after she and David part – confirms her resignation to a convenient isolation. Whereas Winkelman falls to the ground, Karin can at least walk away.

The Madonna symbolism seems too forced to enhance the meaning of the film. David's team uncovers a wooden statue of Madonna and child from a wall in the thirteenth-century church. Sudden exposure to light sets off a decomposition of the statue by hitherto dormant woodworm. We are tempted to see the Madonna (an institutionalized figure) as Karin, corroding through contact with David (a foreign body), but it is too obvious to be an effective symbol. We might suggest to Bergman what Kurt tells the Captain in *The Dance of Death*: 'You've described your hell so realistically that metaphors, however poetic, are out of the picture.' The image does, however, support the contrast between an immemorial cultural-spiritual heritage and the functional novelty of Karin's home. It also provides for a tentative renewal of traditional religious values in Bergman's work.

Bergman skilfully highlights this contrast. Karin's house is bright and colourful but quite characterless. Everything, from *décor* to flower garden, is light and airy. At night the house is cosy; one scene – of Andreas and Karin together – is shot in a golden hue, with emphasis on soft bedroom fabrics. Bergman then cuts to David leaving the church. The dominant colours now are the black and white of a snowy landscape. David's apartment and the interior of the church are equally stark. Inside the church, the mood is sombre, strange, supernatural. Yet at times the atmospheric richness verges on glossy sentimentality, especially when we hear music somewhat in the style of Claude Lelouch. One instance is when Karin reads her poem to David by candlelight with snow falling outside the window. Such sensuousness reminds us of the Hollywood interests in the film. With a brand name here or there and 'muzak' to match, some of the domestic scenes (breakfast, Karin cleaning or laundering) might pass for polished television commercials. Even the credit sequence suggests a Gotland travelogue, while the narration of letters by Karin and David has neither the icy force of the typewritten close-ups in *A Passion*, nor the riveting pathos of Märta's 'recital' in *Winter Light*.

These apparent concessions to commercial vogue are counterbalanced by further proof of Bergman's unusual sensitivity to natural sound and intermittent silence. These elements bolster the fatalistic mood of the film. Three scenes particularly come to mind:

1. the opening sequence, when Karin sees her dead mother in the hospital. Bergman pits the bustle of the outside world against the stillness of the room, stressing human transience and material durability. As Karin gazes on her mother, a noisy bus in the street intrudes on a silence otherwise broken only by a ticking clock. Within this limbo we see isolated close-ups of family photographs, the dead woman's hands, her spectacles on the table, immobile respiratory apparatus, and Karin's stunned expression.

2. when Karin returns home in the morning after getting her family off to school and work. The silence reveals the emptiness of her protective cocoon.

3. when she finds David's apartment empty. He has gone without warning, leaving only their correspondence in a drawer. The place is lifeless, its heavy silence broken only by Karin's sobs and the searing noise of a mechanical saw in an adjacent yard, an unnerving aural symbol of her own cut-up life.

We can identify more readily with the characters in *The Touch* than with the eccentric recluses of earlier isolation dramas. Yet this greater proximity to 'normality' carries with it a debilitating gesture to the mass audience. Bergman brings the problem of isolation disturbingly close to us all, however, in this fascinating but incomplete film.

Cries and Whispers

With this film, Bergman went in for another American collaboration but reverted to Swedish language and cast, dropping the
ubiquitous Max von Sydow and Bibi Andersson. The spirit of
Strindberg is present again in the setting of this cinematic chamber
play on a country estate towards the turn of the century. *Cries and
Whispers* is an outstanding formal achievement. Bergman has never
shown more absolute control of his material; the photography is
exquisite, the acting impeccable; his direction is imaginative,
rigorous and precise, creating a fluid interplay of exterior and
interior, past and present, sound and silence.

The four women around whom the film revolves all suffer from
physical and mental isolation. Three sisters — Agnes, Karin and
Maria — live with their maidservant Anna at the family seat. Agnes
is dying of cancer. They are cut off from the local community
except for occasional visits from the priest and doctor. The film
reminds us constantly of the sisters' status as daughters and wives
of gentry. They lead a timeless, leisured existence indicative of
social and economic privilege. Abundant food and drink, tasteful
furnishings and fine clothes attest to their material comfort. Yet
we sense a decadent class clinging to an existence bereft of former
dignity and grandeur. Bergman captures the aura of the period by
focusing on characteristic, now antique, objects; in one sequence,
to the accompaniment of a music box, we see a doll's house, with
which we associate the historical value of a fading craftsman
culture. This relationship between permanence and disappearance
brings to mind the statue in *The Touch*, the mural in *The Seventh
Seal*, the puppet theatre in *Hour of the Wolf* and, above all, the
wistful scene in *Shame* when, on the eve of civil anarchy, the
Rosenbergs admire a beautiful Meissen ornament belonging to
their wine purveyor. Bergman knows how to make strong political
points without resort to ideological commitment. The fact that his
isolation films thus remain acute but impartial diagnoses of significant political transformations is clearly a double-edged attribute.

The political aspect of *Cries and Whispers* emerges most clearly in the mistress-servant relationship. Anna is far more devoted to Agnes than either Karin or Maria. Yet Karin treats her with acrid condescension, on one occasion striking her for staring in a mirror while she patiently undresses her mistress. Anna proudly refuses Karin's apology with a silent shake of the head, in the circumstances, a much more effective gesture than defiant, retaliatory speech or action.

After Agnes dies, the sisters and their husbands discuss Anna's future. They decide to give her notice and agree somewhat reluctantly to offer her a small bonus. Summoning her, they invite her also to choose a memento of Agnes, which she makes to refuse, prompting a patronizing aside in German from Karin's severe husband Fredrik, designed no doubt to impress on Anna the educated superiority of her employers. Years of loyal service end in the hurried exchange of banknotes and formal farewells, as the squabbling sisters and their husbands leave ceremoniously, their total disrespect of Anna apparent in Karin's remark: 'She's young and strong and has had it very easy up to now.' Anna remains alone in the house, reminding us of Chekhov's *The Cherry Orchard*, where the old valet Firs stays on after the departure of the family (The period and a story of three sisters provide further links with the Russian author).

Agnes is a martyr, her whole life marked by estrangement and pain. A flash-back to her childhood shows fear of her parents and jealousy of her sisters. We see Agnes's mother look at her sorrowfully, in anticipation of later despair and suffering. Agnes also fears her Aunt Olga, a brisk woman who organizes magic lantern shows for the children. When Agnes writes in her diary 'it is early Monday morning and I am in pain', we sense her almost casual resignation to life-long isolation. The final flashback, to an autumn afternoon, shows Agnes in a rare moment of happiness, strolling through the park with Anna and sisters, sitting on a swing, briefly experiencing 'perfection'. However, the memory soon clouds over with a return to illness, hate and fear.

The film reveals a tacit understanding between Anna and Agnes. Although without male partners, their simple love for each other far outweighs the sham marriages of Karin and Maria. Agnes becomes a substitute for Anna's lost child, whose sickness we witness in an early flashback. The spirit of Agnes comes to haunt the house, affecting the three women in different ways. Unlike Karin or Maria, Anna is unafraid to approach the dead woman. Anna symbolically consummates her love in an extended sequence based on her dream of Agnes resurrected. The fantasy is a vehicle for the expression of collective guilt. It starts with Anna hearing a child cry, going to Maria, touching her face and eliciting an inaudible reply. She then waves her hand across Karin's face (recalling the beginning of *Persona*) but gets no response. Finally she goes in to Agnes, who is wearing a baby's bonnet and hovering between life and death. Agnes expresses her anguish in no uncertain terms: 'I can't leave you all. I'm so tired . . . Perhaps for you it's a dream but not for me.' Karin admits her indifference, Maria displays her insincerity ('Oh how sorry I am for you') and, childishly fickle, lets the dead woman's ghost kiss her before running hysterically from the room. Anna, however, cradles Agnes quietly and tenderly; the dream ends.

Tension grows between Karin and Maria after their sister's death, until Karin cries out 'I can't take it any longer. All of that guilt.' Representatives – like Ester and Anna in *The Silence* – of contrasting female personalities, they find it increasingly difficult to coexist with each other. It is notable that as in *Persona*, Bergman tends to shoot their faces in half-light to stress both their hidden and contrasting traits. Karin's social veneer conceals malice and frigidity caused by a miserable marriage. Like the Captain in *The Dance of Death*, Fredrik's 'calcified heart' spreads to Karin, who comes to loathe him and develops an aversion to physical contact, at one point mutilating herself to evade his arrogant advances. Also resisting Maria's playful touch, she screams with horror, succumbing finally to desperate moans and nervous laughter.

Maria is the opposite of Karin: sensual, whimsical, unable to be distant or silent. A flashback shows her affair with the local doctor who, called to Agnes, stays overnight and takes advantage of Maria's forwardness. Dressed seductively in red, she goes to his room, where he gets her to look at herself in a mirror, pointing to her sneer, wrinkles and other signs of 'indifference' and 'easygoing indolent ways.' Yet Maria's chronic vanity prevents her taking the appraisal seriously. Apparently unchangeable, she persists with idle, expedient gestures and words, even ignoring the pathetic pleas of her ineffectual husband Joakin, who attempts suicide on discovering her infidelity. The pervasive 'tissue of lies' obstructs any attempt at reconciliation between the sisters. Maria's opportunistic overtures cause Karin to accuse her of 'falsity' and they part coldly, leaving us feeling that they are, in Strindberg's Captain's words, 'destined to torment one another.'

Cries and Whispers returns to the religious complex that Bergman appeared to solve in the trilogy. *The Touch* hints at renewed concern but contains nothing to match the Lutheran gloom of the funeral scene in *Cries and Whispers*. The priest, played by the elastic-featured Anders Ek in only his third Bergman part in sixteen years, delivers an address reminiscent of speeches by Tomas in *Winter Light* and Albert in *Sawdust and Tinsel*. Albert exclaims 'Poor all of us . . . who live on earth . . . and are so scared' – nineteen years later, Bergman reiterates these doubts and fears: 'Pray for us, who have been left in darkness, left behind on this miserable earth . . . Plead with Him that He may make sense and meaning of our lives . . . She [Agnes] was my confirmation child . . . Her faith was stronger than mine.' It is a remarkable and surprising reprise of a long standing fear. Furthermore the other characters, apart from Anna, share the priest's sentiments; in the bedroom scene the doctor asks Maria 'Is there no absolution for such as you and I?' They are as barren spiritually as their modern counterparts. (*The Rite* – a chronological bridge between *Shame* and *A Passion* – offers a clue to Bergman's revival of religious conscience: Thea Winkelman prays that God may save her soul 'before it perishes in emptiness.') Anna prays and reads the bible, suggesting that the materially deprived adhere to a spiritual existence which affluent society subordinates or rejects. The key to love may lie in renewal of faith. Although we are close again to the false equation of *Through a Glass Darkly*, Bergman no longer forces a connection, preferring to observe admiringly the embodiment in Anna of a basic, spontaneous love.

As befits his concentration on women, Bergman employs long

facial close-ups, especially of Agnes (asleep, her mouth is •wollen like Elisabet's in *Persona*). We watch Karin's hands as she does accounts, while certain shots of Karin and Maria together strongly resemble compositions from *Persona*: a profile two-shot, for instance, without sound in support of moving lips, emphasizes their dismal lack of communication. Bergman also uses Agnes's diary as a source of information: sometimes Agnes narrates, an external narrator twice introduces flashbacks and, towards the end, Anna lights a candle to read (with Agnes's voice over) the extract about the joyful moment in the garden. Bergman's intensive investigation of the female psyche fits his self-definition as an artist who goes 'inside' people. While his incisive vision produces extraordinary women ('a race apart' says Dilys Powell), it enables him to exploit his medium to the utmost.

The film is episodic, with frequent dissolves to effect spatio-temporal transitions. These dissolves are accompanied by those very cries and whispers which betoken the fears and suspicions of the characters. Sometimes Bergman mixes these eerie sounds with the roaring wind, an effect that may derive partly from his reference in the script of *Through a Glass Darkly* to rain beating on a window pane 'like a cry and a whisper,' partly to the breakdown of coherent language in *Persona* into fragmentary sound. The technique creates a sinister atmosphere reminiscent, says John Russell Taylor in *The Times* (9 February 1973), of Maeterlinck 'in its underplayed mysterious beauty'. Natural sound is again crucial – we hear a lot of breathing and clocks (especially early on) and the only music is a little Chopin and Bach for piano and violin respectively.

The colour of the film is dominated by red and white. Most of the dissolves are suffused with a bloody red, symbolic of the widespread physical and mental wounds. Like Maria's dress, the furnishings are mainly red. White symbolizes peace and lost time (in the garden flashback, all the women wear white and carry white parasols) but also Agnes, child and adult, is always in white. On the night of Agnes's deterioration, white lamps flare in dark corridors, a fine example of Nykvist's photographic skill, as in the opening sequence, when a limpid establishing shot – stone statues in a mist — leads us from the garden into virtual entombment within the house. Moreover, as if to define the imaginary experience, Anna's dream replaces the thematic colours with pale blue, grey and green.

In spite of all this cinematic virtuosity, there are serious objections to the film. While we can only admire Bergman's utterly honest treatment of human behaviour, we may wonder how to carry on absorbing such unmitigated exposure to suffering, violence, hate and despair. Peter Cowie once warned: 'At any moment he may overbalance, offend his spectators, and lose his reputation completely' (*Sweden Two*, p. 95). On the face of it this seems unlikely but, after the comparative levity of *The Magic Flute*, he reverts in subsequent films (*Face to Face, The Serpent's Egg* and *Autumn Sonata*) to his painful obsessions. He needs to find a new direction in which all is not hell on earth. He is otherwise in danger of becoming a flawless technician without audience, apart from masochists in search of regular emotional batterings. Yet, in his defence, would he not be dishonest to substitute something unfelt and purely compensatory? He claims that he will eventually give up film-making, yet at the start of the eighties there is no sign of an end to his irrepressible activity. As he says in the script of *Cries and Whispers*: 'All my so-called artistic expression is only a desperate protest against death. Despite this, I keep on . . .' We shall see if he does, and hope that the isolation films are not the powerful but clear admission that Bergman's cinema is at the end of its tether, that he can say no more without repeating himself, or else abandon his art for good.

CHAPTER FOUR

AN UNCERTAIN WORLD

Into Television

Elisabet Vogler's stunned reaction to newsreel violence in *Persona* makes clear Bergman's view of the profound cultural impact of television. It was to be expected that he would eventually, after decades of movie-making, turn to what Marshall McLuhan calls this 'cool, participant medium'. How could he have resisted, indeed, an art form which 'promotes depth structures in art and entertainment alike, and creates audience involvement in depth as well' (McLuhan, *Understanding Media*)? His art took a new direction in *A Passion* with the deliberate decomposition of the photographic image: the grainy close-ups in that film, foreshadowed in *Hour of the Wolf*, no doubt led him to feel he should go right over to a medium which is low-definition *par excellence*; and his abandoning of religious and metaphysical anguish as a theme (*The Silence* being the last great film of that mode) in favour of the almost obsessional probing of personal relationships in films like *Shame, A Passion* and *The Touch*, made an excursion into TV natural and indeed inevitable. He was able to exploit to the full the fact that the TV image, as McLuhan points out, 'is not photo in any sense, but a ceaselessly forming contour of things limned by the scanning-finger', a 'flat two-dimensional mosaic' and sometimes even a 'blur'. The close-up, used in the cinema for shock purposes, is in TV 'a quite casual thing', and facial reactions are what the spectator concentrates upon as a matter of instinct; it is therefore, McLuham argues, the medium encouraging the most immediate and intimate audience participation.

In spite of this, Bergman's first essay in television, his black comedy *The Rite*, was not a particularly subtle or indeed successful use of the medium. It tells how a touring group of three actors are accused of obscenity and hailed before a local magistrate. Like the magician in *The Face* they enact a ritual to terrify the magistrate, but in this more sombre version of the story they actually strike him dead by the power of suggestion of their 'rite'. In a world from which God has withdrawn, Gavin Millar comments, 'the artist's illusions are the nearest we shall get to a miracle'. 'Outside the frail ring of human warmth', the magistrate (a 'sort of lay St Peter') remarks, 'there is only cruelty, for ever and ever'. This bleak and claustrophobic film — the medium of TV is not alone responsible for the small cast and the oppressive atmosphere and restricted locale — is overshadowed by *Hour of the Wolf* which is a richer and more disturbing exploration of the same theme: the artist's responsibility for his nightmares.

Bergman's second TV play, *Reservatet*, is harder to assess because the only form in which it has been seen by British audiences is in an English adaptation entitled *The Lie*, directed by Alan Bridges and played by Joss Ackland, Frank Finlay and Gemma Jones. But even seen in a remote form it was evident that there was a flaw in the conception of the central female character, who was neither fully a social/professional butterfly, nor a wife rent by conflicting feelings as in *The Touch*; and whereas in other Bergman works the particular anguish of the torn couple is seen in a context of wider, even metaphysical doubt and dread, here there was no 'frame', and as such it lacked depth and perspective. Nevertheless, in its exploration of the way human beings live by lies — or more precisely, shelter, often unconsciously, behind 'reservations' and other forms of truth-withholding — it foreshadowed in miniature the theme and treatment of *Scenes from a Marriage*; in both works, for instance, there is a cathartically violent physical struggle when the 'lie' by which the protagonists live is revealed to them, mutually and simultaneously.

Reservatet was followed by *Faro Document* which has already been touched upon briefly in connection with its interesting combination of highly-stylized episodes in colour cut in with almost *cinéma-vérité* sequences in black and white; it is also notable for a characteristically ominous guitar or violin-string twang (echoed and amplified) used to conclude sections. Although (like *The Rite*,

Scenes from a Marriage, The Magic Flute and *Face to Face*), it has been issued also as a cinema film, it is naturally not particularly successful in such a context. After seeing *Scenes from a Marriage* (film version) Gavin Millar quite understandably found it 'a bit of a visual disappointment' and even thought it 'blown up 16mm material'. Reviewing the six-episode original TV version, another critic, Michael Ratcliffe, acknowledged that the shortened copy showed 'distinct signs of structural clumsiness', but he had nothing but praise for the full-length work.

Scenes from a Marriage was written, Bergman claims, to give himself pleasure and not, at least at the outset, with television in mind at all. He started with the third story ('Paula') and thinking that he would like to know more about the characters, wrote episodes two, one, six, four and finally five (the most harrowing and violent), in that order. The published script only provides the bare narrative bones of the work, with little or no reference to decor. It is, however, sharp and vivid.

The story is a deliberately banal one of a happy and contented middle-class Swedish marriage, bearing analogies with the marriage in *The Touch*. But whereas in that film the marriage was disrupted by an outsider, in *Scenes from a Marriage* it collapses under its own internal tensions (like those of Karin and Maria in *Cries and Whispers*). The dramatic line is very similar to that in *Shame*: things start off well and gradually go from bad to worse. Unlike *Shame*, however, there is a slight rise in hope and expectation at the end.

In the first part of the playlet, Johan and Marianne are conventional and set in their ways. They are, they think, blissfully and uncomplicatedly happy in their marriage and in their professional lives. They have two children, with whom their relationship is quite uncomplicated. In the second part everything is still ideal, 'almost splendid'. But the basic tensions are becoming more evident, and the scene as a whole is significantly entitled 'the art of sweeping under the rug'.

It is in the third part, 'Paula', that the blow falls. Johan announces rather brutally that he is in love with another woman and is going to live with her. Again, to preserve their carefully built dignity, Marianne controls herself, breaking down only when

he leaves. In the fourth part, entitled 'The Vale of Tears', Johan returns to Marianne. Things not going well with the mistress, he suggests that he should return. But Marianne, rather like the heroine (played by Jill Clayburgh) of Mazursky's *An Unmarried Woman*, will not take him back. She is gradually acquiring confidence in her new role as an independent woman. But she is not yet fully on top of things, and this coupled with Johan's palpable weakness entitles Bergman to describe this as 'a very sad scene'.

In the fifth part there is a terrible row, culminating in violent behaviour when the two (like Andreas and Anna in *A Passion*) physically attack each other and Marianne is brutally beaten up by Johan. As Bergman puts it, 'they want to destroy one another, and they very nearly succeed'. When the fight is over, they both sign the divorce papers, formally ending their marriage. As she leaves with the documents, Marianne says significantly: 'We should have started fighting long ago. It would have been much better'.

The sixth and last part is entitled 'In the Middle of the Night in a Dark House Somewhere in the World'. Marianne, now re-married, is much more confident and outgoing. She is shown in the first part of the scene learning to talk to her mother intimately for the first time: as she says, 'you and I have never talked like this before'. We then see Johan, who has also remarried (though not apparently to the original mistress Paula), and is ending an affair with yet another mistress, Eva. She and a colleague of his are intrigued to know whom he has taken up with now, to explain his breaking in this way with Eva. They all think it is his secretary Lena, but the audience knows better, and soon is confirmed in its suspicion that the new 'mistress' is in fact Marianne herself. They have been meeting each other secretly on and off for some time. When the series opened, they had been married for ten years: in this last scene, twenty years have passed. Now 'released', they find their 'illicit' meetings intensely exciting both sexually and emotionally, especially since the torture they were inflicting on each other is now well behind them. In this last scene, they recall their first clandestine meeting after the divorce:

JOHAN: I was awfully pleased actually.

Stills from *Scenes from a Marriage*

> MARIANNE: And I was pleased that you were pleased.
> JOHAN: And you said right off, let's get out of here and go back to my place. My husband's away and won't be home until Friday.
> MARIANNE: You blushed.
> JOHAN: You bet your sweet life I did. I got such a hard-on that I could hardly stand up straight.
> MARIANNE (*Smiling*): It was nothing to the way I felt.

They also talk about each other's marriages, and it is clear that they are both conventionally happy. But it is also apparent that their own links have never been truly severed; if anything, their relationship has finally entered a mature stage. Having borrowed a friend's cottage for the weekend, they eventually 'snuggle down' together in bed, and end up with an extraordinarily conjugal conversation which closes the whole sequence of plays:

> MARIANNE; Good night, my darling. And thanks for the talk.
> JOHAN: Good night.
> MARIANNE: Sleep well.
> JOHAN: Thanks, the same to you.
> MARIANNE: Good night.

On this banal but moving note Bergman ends his penetrating analysis of the tensions between two people who remain linked for life, even though they have gone through numerous vicissitudes on the legal and formal level. In other words, *Scenes from a Marriage* is a study of marriage both in the legal sense of the official tie, and in the metaphysical and even mystical sense of the sacrament between two human beings of which the church speaks. Although Bergman is no longer a believer, and although the plays are sexually outspoken to a marked degree, and although, too, the events described would shock a puritan, since the protagonists are fairly promiscuous, nonetheless the basic point that these two are joined forever is borne out through their moments of happiness in the early part, their moments of extreme degradation in the middle (which go far beyond anything Edward Albee demonstrated in

Who's Afraid of Virginia Woolf), and their relative calm and peace at the end, when they have become somehow 'citizens of the world of reality in quite a different way from before'. This last comment is Bergman's; uncharacteristically, he has written a preface to the published version of the play, as he himself says, contrary to his habit. It consists of a commentary on the six scenes, which develops and amplifies in a discursive manner the dramatic action set out in the dialogue.

The series was extraordinarily successful on Swedish television; it kept practically the whole country at home. Streets were deserted, appointments cancelled, while everyone followed this moving and terrifying story which might well have been their own. Bergman had never known mass popularity like this before, and one can see why it was so immensely gripping. Bergman is often accused of writing banal dialogue, and one can criticize certain details of these scripts, as for instance, his clumsy use of an interviewer, who happens to be an old school friend of Marianne and who presents in the first scene the complacent happiness of the marriage. But in spite of minor flaws, the writing is of great incisiveness, particularly as the momentum develops. A great deal of the dialogue must come from personal experience, and its deadly accuracy cannot fail to remind the spectator of things he or she has thought or said. Moreover, Bergman is able to modulate with extraordinary skill, from lyricism to banality, and from moments of infinite tenderness to actions of extreme cruelty. The whole pathos of life, in which people are unable to apply the laws of reason to the anarchy of their emotional lives – a situation we are all faced with – is poignantly brought out in this work.

In the television play, Marianne is acted, as one might expect, by Liv Ullmann; since part of the message is that she is, for all her professional achievements as a family lawyer, basically a child at heart, the casting is evidently perfect. Johan is acted by Erland Josephson, who took the part of Elis in *A Passion* and the doctors in both *Cries and Whispers* and *Face to Face*. He, too, is presented as a vulnerable man, even, as he puts it himself, 'a child with genitals, a fabulous combination when it comes to women with maternal feelings' (p. 187). Revealingly, Bergman states that 'this opus took three months to write, but rather a long part of my life to experience'. Although it is not directly autobiographical, it clearly represents the harvest of a life-time of association with women. And once again, women come out best in this work; Marianne, for all her basic infantilism, is a better, a stronger, a more lucid and, morally, a more attractive person than Johan. He is not as pusillanimous as Johan in *Shame*, but nor is he the virile and professionally successful all-rounder that he would wish to maintain and project as his image.

What Bergman's television plays all have in common is a largely indoor locale and a small cast, as one would expect; they use the medium's limitations to positive effect (in the film version the constant close-ups of *Scenes from a Marriage* eventually become oppressive to the eye, whereas they are natural in the original copy). Bergman once said that he dreams of making a fixed camera film (an idea already explored, characteristically, by some independent filmmakers) which would maintain interest in one face for up to two hours. He has obviously not gone as far as that: in fact, with its deliberate narrative jumps, the composition of *Scenes from a Marriage* is highly sophisticated. But as always with Bergman the technical skills serve a vision: in this instance the portrayal of a world 'in which anything is possible because nothing really matters' (Michael Ratcliffe), and of people whose behaviour is continually at variance with their language. In other words, the classic Bergman issues, which are matters of anguish for him and for the rest of us.

The Problem of Isolation

As we have seen, the effect of isolation on thought and action is evident even in early works like *Summer Interlude, Waiting Women* and *Summer with Monika*, with the Stockholm archipelago as setting for blends of idyllic and tragic solitude. There is, at this stage, no integral connection between physical isolation and a character's state of mind; such locations function mainly as temporary breaks ('interlude', 'waiting', 'summer') from the workaday world. A deliberate indentification of physical with mental isolation becomes apparent in *Through a Glass Darkly*, whereafter most of Bergman's work revolves around the chronic inability of a series of individuals to deal with personal and social difficulties. In these films, isolated environments correspond directly to the psychological problems of their inhabitants. This tendency reaches a peak in *A Passion* and, while the idea of isolation continues to concern Bergman, he now approaches it from a somewhat less explicit angle. The intensification of personal isolation follows on a rejection of religious faith and a reinforcement of materialistic values, growing almost without exception from *The Silence* to *Face to Face*.

Bergman utilizes his former home on the Baltic island of Fårö to depict isolation in *Hour of the Wolf*, *Shame*, and *A Passion*. He feels an awesome elemental force in the lonely landscape and seascape but also a peaceful contrast to the complex and complacent artifice of urban society and the welfare state. Bergman tells A. Alvarez in an interview:

> If I am angry and go out to the beach and scream,
> perhaps some silly bird flies up from a tree. But if I
> come into the studio and scream, there will be an
> enormous explosion and everyone will talk about it. So
> I can get an absolutely wrong idea of my importance.
> On the island, nobody cares.

His last remark is deeply ironic: on one hand, it describes a freedom to release one's own pent-up feelings; on the other hand, it confirms the heartless indifference of his isolated characters to the feelings of others.

Most of Bergman's isolated individuals are newcomers to the area, invariably artists or professionals seeking some peace and quiet. Thus he suggests that they arrive already 'isolated' in some way and that life on the island only accentuates their fears and weaknesses. The poor, hard-working natives do not, significantly, share this mental isolation; they are simple people at one with their surroundings.

Bergman generally portrays his isolated individuals as narcissistic and insincere. This is one reason for their unhappiness; another is their sense of an overall cultural despair. Indeed, their social and intellectual backgrounds render them particularly vulnerable to this contagious, malignant malaise. Unfortunately it implicates everyone including the natives, whose relative unawareness is insufficient protection against its manifestations, as in the case of Jonas Persson in *Winter Light* or, in the island films, old Johan in *A Passion*. Poet and peasant, priest and pauper, all suffer from disillusionment with the traditional strength of culture, church and community. Increasing exposure to public violence, vulgarity and pretence forces sensitive people into evasive action, non-commitment, silence and retreat. Some, like Elis Vergerus in *A Passion*, hide cynically behind their affluence; others, terrified and helpless, cower in corners (Winkelman='cornerman'). According to the Primal Therapist, Arthur Janov:

> Perhaps the civilization process itself makes human beings so uncivilized to one another, producing frustration and hostility. Being civilized too often means being in control of one's feelings, and this control may be the source of inner rage.
>
> (*The Primal Scream*, p. 322)

Janov's words accord with Bergman's admission that one of his 'life-problems' is his constant 'rage'. This rage may, if misdirected, cause guilt, panic or hurt. The trouble is, Bergman tells Alvarez, 'everybody has forgotten love but, inside, everybody remembers the law'. This anarchic, amoral slide – a concomitant of social and economic failure – has become, with the influential aid of the mass media, an uneasy part of our daily experience. Bergman cannot foresee redemption:

> Our social behaviour patterns ... have proved a fiasco ... The tragic thing is, we neither can nor want to, nor have the strength to alter course ... Just around the corner an insect world is waiting for us – and one day it's going to roll in over our ultra-individualized existence.
>
> (*Bergman on Bergman*, p. 18)

The artist/intellectual – once an avatar, an 'unacknowledged legis-lator' – feels this depression most acutely. Mass media, especially television, have taken dramatic creativity largely out of the artist's hands, leaving him to pursue his own ideological allegiances, aesthetic fetishes or desperate solipsisms. Writing in the Danish film magazine *Kosmorama*, Niels Jensen traces the problem to Romanticism, 'when art lost its prized function of serving ecclesiastical or secular authorities and instead became an instru-ment for the sensitive individual's personal development.' Berg-man, showing his admiration for the anonymous builders of Chartres cathedral, goes further back, to the separation of art from religion in the Renaissance.

Should we then excuse these superfluous figures their faults, as victims of false social priorities? There is, after all, a telling ambiguity in Bergman's comment in Winkelman's collapse: 'that man hasn't a chance of existing in the material world' (*Bergman on Bergman*, p.255). Moreover, wrote Ingemar Hedenius in 1961:

> Our penniless artists constitute a capital that is lying idle. Subsidies and grants will not suffice to make it productive. We need fresh ideas of what it means to lead a dignified human life.
>
> (*Sweden Writes*, p. 220)

His last sentence is fairly consistent with Bergman's isolation films but although, as George Steiner says, 'our pessimistic vision ... has neither a rationale of causality nor a hope of transcendent remission' (*In Bluebeard's Castle*, p.65), the various portraits offered by Bergman do not wholly absolve his characters from blame. In fact, these films suggest that it is immoral to take refuge in art, seclusion, or both. Bergman reiterates that personal isola-tion is dangerous and reprehensible because it is both cowardly and an illusory security. The greater our disengagement from the community at large, the greater our self-deception and the harsher the experience which shatters that illusion. Witness Pastor Tomas, David, Alma and Elisabet, the Borgs, the Rosenbergs, Winkel-man. Bergman's points about isolation invite comparison with, for example, Peckinpah's film *Straw Dogs*, which also links isolation with an unforeseen eruption of violence. *Straw Dogs* depicts the gruesome consequences of an individual's wilful detachment from a rural community that for generations has taken interdependence for granted. Cornwall replaces Fårö but the message is identical: a tragic breakdown of community in the modern world. As in Peckinpah's film, Bergman's 'isolationists,' trapped by forces beyond their control, succumb to their own as well as to others' baser instincts.

This nonplussed state betrays a complete lack of conviction on the part of the 'isolationists'. Their egocentric existence blinds or hardens them to the needs and wishes of others. Bergman always shies at the idea of political commitment, preferring his films to make their own points. Yet Swedish neutralism – 'poison', says Bergman – clearly has a deleterious effect on, for instance, the Rosenbergs, or Winkelman and his neighbours, while in *The Touch* one reason for Karin Vergerus's attraction to the impulsive David Kovac is her weariness with a comfortable bourgeois niche. Yet David is equally isolated by his rootlessness. Their relationship ultimately breaks down because both are bound by their respective backgrounds. Karin becomes acutely conscious of what Ingemar Hedenius calls the 'latent antagonism between this ideal (utilitarian welfare state) and a religious . . . attitude to life' (*Sweden Writes*, p. 213), while David suffers from the social nonentity of a wandering Jew. In this film – as in *A Passion, Cries and Whispers* and *Scenes from a Marriage* – political implications emerge automatically and naturally from Bergman's penetrating critiques of different ways of life.

Although Bergman's recent pessimism seems unrelenting, he seeks alternatives – however tentative or questionable – to the human impasse reached in *A Passion*. He gains some relief from the pervasive gloom of his isolation theme by revealing the strength of love between, for instance, Karin and David in *The Touch*, or Anna and Agnes in *Cries and Whispers*. These glimmers of honesty, heart and hope – completely absent from *Shame* or *A Passion* – prove that while Bergman despairs, he is by no means a misanthropist, revelling in the discomfort of mankind.

Faro Document is interesting in that Bergman opts for a

documentary analysis, in this case not of the neurotic sophisticates of *A Passion* (which it follows) but rather of the native population, a disorganized and exploited sector of Swedish society. Yet although Bergman's political indignation is clear, he stresses the qualities and talents of this community, relatively untouched as it is by the pressures of contemporary life. The natives respond intuitively to their environment and possess an age-old capacity for cooperation and coexistence. In bringing out the intrinsic merit of their life style, Bergman attributes their social problems more to the failure of the state to respect their opinions, rights and needs than to the defects in their own traditions. His decision to make the film may also be a means of expiating a guilty awareness that his island life – like that of Winkelman and his friends – represents what Steiner calls 'the ontological imbalance ... between the privileged locale of intellectual and artistic achievement, and the excluded world of poverty and underdevelopment' (p. 68). *Faro Document* thus reflects an ambiguity: on the one hand, Bergman points to the island's social and material backwardness as an embarrassment to the state but, on the other hand, he suggests – especially in the light of his isolation films – that the inhabitants may be better off without the dubious benefits of advanced civilization.

Scenes from a Marriage summarizes the isolation theme from the vantage point of a demanding urban existence. The settings shift from *The Touch* (a small island town) to *Cries and Whispers* (a country estate) to *Scenes from a Marriage* (Stockholm). Nonetheless, the anguished remarks of Johan and Marianne place them firmly on the familiar 'island' of personal turmoil:

> Our whole life is mapped out into little squares.
> (*Scenes from a Marriage*, p. 43)

> Both you and I have escaped into an existence that has been hermetically sealed. (p. 90)

> Can the scheme of things be so treacherous that life suddenly goes wrong? Without your knowing how it happens. Almost imperceptibly. (p. 64)

I'm a failure and I'm going downhill and I'm scared . . .
(p. 150)

Do you think we're living in utter confusion . . . The
whole lot of us? (p. 196)

Their sentiments noticeably recall those of Winkelman and Anna
Fromm in *A Passion*. Johan and Marianne are isolated in their
marriage, social circle, work and language. Marianne, ironically a
divorce lawyer, is staggered by a client's description of emotional
isolation, a condition towards which Marianne realizes she may
also be heading:

> MRS JACOBI: I tell myself that I have the capacity for
> love, but it's all bottled up inside me. The trouble is
> that the life I have lived up to now has . . . stifled my
> potentialities . . . (p. 54)

The idea of isolation through language recurs in this film.
Marianne describes another unhappy couple, their friends Karin
and Peter:

> They don't speak the same language. They must trans-
> late into a third language they both understand in order
> to get each other's meaning . . .

She adds:

> I'm always coming across it in my work. Sometimes it's
> as if husband and wife were making a long-distance call
> to one another on faulty telephones. Sometimes it's like
> hearing two tape recorders with preset programs.
> (p. 25)

These observations apply equally to their own marriage, which
suffers from their failure to communicate openly with each other.
They try to discuss their problems but succumb too often to
sarcasm and defensiveness. Above all, Marianne tells Johan of a
dream of isolation, like those of Eva in *Shame* and Anna in *A
Passion*:

> We have to go along a dangerous road or something . . .

At that moment I am slithering in soft sand. I can't
reach you. You're all standing up there on the road and
I can't reach you. (p. 195)

A few years later the estranged couple spend a weekend together
but it is a fleeting reunion. Both have remarried and found some
relief from their former isolation:

JOHAN: ... I think I've found my right proportions.
And ... I've accepted my limitations with a certain
humility. (p. 183)
MARIANNE: ... Why are we telling the truth now? I
know. It's because we make no demands. (p. 183)

Such relative peace of mind is totally lacking in *A Passion* but, for
all that, it remains Bergman's most exquisite view of the problem
of isolation. It is a disturbingly pertinent appraisal of life in the
Western world but also a demonstration of cinematic virtuosity.
The uncertain pessimistic ending testifies to the film's utter integrity.

We sense Bergman's desire to explore fresh territory after *A
Passion*, yet with the exception of *The Magic Flute* — a radiant
diversion — he has not managed to transcend the intense pessimism
of his island dramas. *The Touch* has fine moments unfortunately
offset by commercial compromise, while *Cries and Whispers* is
technically flawless but unpalatably harrowing. *Face to Face* once
more articulates the bleakness of individual despair. Liv Ullmann,
as Jenny Isaksson, a psychiatrist who succumbs to mental breakdown then bungles a suicide attempt, gives a no-holds-barred
performance supported by other familiar faces, notably those of
Erland Josephson as her doctor friend Tomas Jacobi, and Gunnar
Björnstrand as her senile grandfather. Yet even if *Cries and Whispers*
and *Scenes from a Marriage* are fairly uncompromising films, *Face to
Face* goes overboard in its relentless probing of psychic pain. Many
riveting close-ups show Bergman's continued interest in the potential of televisual material but the force of these shots is insufficient
to offset the glaring faults of the film: psychological self-
indulgence, heavy-handed symbolism, facile coda and excessive

length. It is altogether too familiar an emotional assault on the faithful Bergman spectator.

In *A Passion*, we can readily identify with Andreas and Anna as they sit in frustration at their tables, as in *Shame* with Jan and Eva's pathetic attempt to preserve their sheltered life. Many of us also know or discover, like Johan and Marianne in *Scenes from a Marriage*, how physical violence may explode in personal relationships. But it is almost impossible to identify with Jenny because of the sheer extremity both of her mental derangement and of her physical condition following the attempted suicide. In other words, the individual or social complexes which cause neurosis are recognizable by much of Bergman's audience but, fortunately, few can relate genuinely to the distances of psychosis. Where Bergman previously depicts insanity, he makes fewer demands on the spectator and — paradoxically perhaps — the treatment is more satisfactory; in *Through a Glass Darkly*, we are made fully aware of Karin's schizophrenic identity but the exposure is brief, allowing us an effective glimpse of an essentially inaccessible experience; in *Hour of the Wolf*, we witness extensive visualization of Johan's frightful hallucinations but remain nonetheless at a suitable remove, partly because of the analytical framework set up in the prologue, and partly because the 'gothicizing' of his fantasies establishes for us an acceptable aesthetic mode.

Such artistic control is lacking in *Face to Face*. Although the use of fades (as in *Cries and Whispers*) ensures smooth transitions between Jenny's 'real' and dream worlds, the number of excursions into one or the other of these worlds results in severe overstatement of theme, as well as an awkward and unrestrained mixture of naturalistic and surrealistic imagery. Unlike, for instance, in *Wild Strawberries* or *Persona*, Bergman fails here to combine these oscillating 'realities' within a satisfying emotional and intellectual whole. The film sinks into a seemingly endless parade of gruesome experiences as Jenny confronts her disturbed past. Bergman's preface to the script suggests that Jenny is basically an uncomfortable projection of his own desire for self-exorcism: 'After having given my anxiety various labels, each less convincing than the other, I decided to begin investigating more methodically'

(*Face to Face*, p. v). Indeed, this is the problem – the film is so unnervingly methodical in its madness that ultimately we perceive little beyond a highly personal confession couched in extravagant sequences and filtered through a set of stereotypical characters.

Face to Face is another isolation film but this time Bergman labours his message. As Philip Strick points out (*Sight and Sound*, Winter 1976-77), Bergman 'shuffles the well-worn cards and lays them out once more'. Moreover, in its almost unmitigated sense of suffering, the film places an unreasonable strain on the spectator. The lighter patches are too self-consciously grafted on to the unhealthy skin to be truly redemptive or even provide adequate relief. As in *Through a Glass Darkly*, the ending makes an unconvincing appeal to the power of love and devotion; Jenny's final perception of her grandparents' 'all-embracing' but quite exclusive love for each other seems a hurried afterthought which does little or nothing to restore our shattered illusions. It is as if Bergman, after a selfish spree, feels guilty and makes a late, forced gesture to those whom he has understandably repulsed. When he says in the preface (p. v) that the film 'deals ("as usual", I was about to say!) with Life, Love and Death', the exclamation mark suggests a nervous laugh, an embarrassed hint of an artistic rut.

During her agonizing recovery, Jenny asks Tomas 'Do you think I'm crippled for the rest of my life? Do you think we're a vast army of emotionally crippled wretches wandering about calling to each other with words which we don't understand and which only make us even more afraid?' (p. 105).

This serves as perfect expression of the isolation theme in Bergman's recent career – it could easily be Andreas Winkelman talking to Anna Fromm. But *Face to Face* is an unwelcome regurgitation of that motif, which no longer strikes with the chilling force of *Shame* or *A Passion*. The film is a tiresome reprise of Bergman's favourite themes: death as a horror, the thin line between love and hate, between waking and dreaming, and man as a forlorn being trapped, as Jenny says (p. 64), 'in an isolation that has got worse and worse'. As for placing this theme in a new context of female suicide, we need only look back to *Prison* or *Thirst* for confirmation of its former appearance. As Henry Chapier says (*Combat*, 8 Sep-

Stills from *Face to Face*

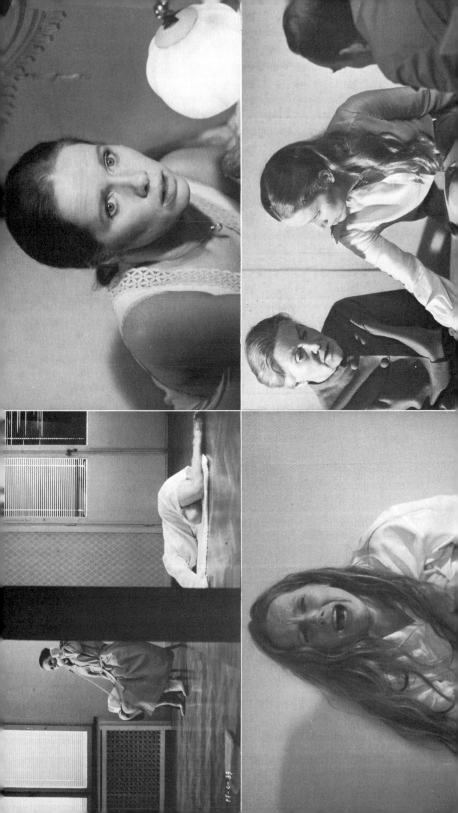

tember 1970), 'in becoming the icy expression of his bitter philosophy, the cinema of Bergman ... inspires only respect'. With *Face to Face*, I fear that even this respect suffers a blow, compounding my concluding misgivings about *Cries and Whispers*.

Since *Face to Face*, Bergman has made two more films, *The Serpent's Egg* and *Autumn Sonata*. *The Serpent's Egg*, an idea dating back to 1965, does mark something of a departure in being Bergman's first film made outside Sweden – it was made in Germany – and is one of three features in a deal between Bergman and the Hollywood-based producer Dino de Laurentiis. This wider enterprise shows in the international cast: David Carradine plays Abel Rosenberg, a confused and down-at-heel American-Jewish circus artiste, supported by a largely German cast, with only Nykvist as photographer and Liv Ullmann (as Abel's sister-in-law Manuela) from the regular Swedish retinue.

The action takes place in Berlin in the November week in 1923 when the Deutschmark exploded and Hitler, in the wake of his abortive Munich putsch, wrote *Mein Kampf* in jail. Utilising a studio location reminiscent in its street scenes of *The Silence*, *The Serpent's Egg* is equally Kafkaesque in atmosphere, 'showing' says Philip Strick, 'a society in wild confusion and dread, where lives are shattered by the arbitrary malice of unknown controllers' (*Sight and Sound*, Summer 1978), a situation more than likely reflecting Bergman's own recent bitter experience of faceless authority. Bergman doubtless intends a comparison between his historical setting and the state of the contemporary Western world, choosing as an epigraph to the script Georg Büchner's assertion that 'man is an abyss and I turn giddy when I look down into it'. This view is reinforced by Abel's circus friend, Hollinger, who reads aloud from a newspaper that 'existence today seems to be nothing else but being full of dread' (*The Serpent's Egg*, p. 10), while Abel maintains that 'tomorrow the abyss will open and everything will vanish in a final catastrophe' (p. 42). The film recycles familiar Bergman elements: we see film clips of extreme suffering; we witness joint prayer – in the manner of *Winter Light* – between diffident priest and desperate supplicant; we hear utterances of anguish and fear that might as easily have come from any one of Bergman's tortured

Stills from *The Serpent's Egg*

protagonists. The film is often reminiscent – indeed almost derivative – of *Cabaret* (for the set of which Bergman's designer, Rolf Zehetbauer, shared an Oscar) yet, although visually striking, it has neither the verve and breadth of Fosse's film, nor the psychological subtlety of Fassbinder's *Despair*, another film dealing – more obliquely – with the decadence of pre-Nazi Germany.

The second of Bergman's films made outside Sweden, *Autumn Sonata* enjoyed British financial support and, like *The Serpent's Egg*, was produced in Germany. Shot in Norway, the film marks not only Bergman's fairly rapid return to a depressingly familiar middle-class Scandinavian context, but also the reappearance in the Swedish-speaking cinema of Ingrid Bergman. She plays Charlotte, a famous concert pianist and mother of Eva (Liv Ullmann), the quiet, unselfish wife of a country parson.

The film concerns Charlotte's first visit in seven years to her daughter's house. Charlotte's decision to come is, one feels, primarily to help her over the death of Leonardo, her long-standing musical companion. Bergman apparently had for some years toyed with the idea of making a film about the relationship between a woman and her daughter, in particular the problem (stemming from their education, Bergman surmises) of women's repression of aggressive feelings. Tension between the two women – compounded by Charlotte's guilty embarrassment on learning that her spastic daughter Lena is living in the house – gradually builds through a series of goads and veiled accusations until, predictably, the dam bursts and meek little Eva lets fly:

> You never listen ... you're a notorious escapist ... you're emotionally crippled ... you detest me and Helena, because you're hopelessly shut up inside yourself...
>
> *(Autumn Sonata*, p. 61)

The film is another episode in Bergman's hell of private lives, although he deals forcefully with the problem of a child living in the shadow of an ambitious and successful parent. In one revealing scene, Eva plays a Chopin prelude for her mother. Charlotte first compliments Eva evasively, then, provoked by Eva's reaction,

launches into a technical criticism of the interpretation before
consenting to play the piece ceremoniously, disdainful yet nervous
of Eva's response. Bergman skilfully depicts the mutual fear,
insensitivity and misunderstanding beneath a veneer of cultured
deference. 'The performance was superb' remarks Eva ironically to
her husband Viktor; the guilty 'act' of the artist clearly plagues
Bergman no less today than in a film like *The Face* made more than
twenty years ago.

Philip French (*The Observer*, 19 November 1978) detects a
stylistic throwback to Bergman's trilogy, and the rural parish
setting is reminiscent of *Winter Light*. In fact, *Autumn Sonata* is a
tissue of similarities with earlier works; only the package is new.
The element of isolation recurs at a basic level, while the intimate
confessions and subsequent hostility between the two women
bring *Persona* to mind; the retiring existence of Eva and Viktor
recalls the Rosenbergs in *Shame*; Charlotte's description of
Leonardo's hospital death is very close in mood to Karin's experience of her mother's death in *The Touch*; and the somewhat morbid
references to the couple's drowned three-year old Erik has a familiar
ring (for example, reminiscent of Nicholas Roeg's *Don't Look Now*).
The struggle to use the 'right words' reminds us of David in
Through a Glass Darkly, a film in which there was a conclusion as
emotionally and dramatically suspect as that of *Autumn Sonata*. At
one point Eva tells Charlotte that 'there can be no forgiveness'
(p. 71), yet the final written attempt at a reconciliation with her
mother is a clear case of locking the stable door after the horse has
bolted. Charlotte packs and leaves as suddenly as she had arrived,
returning to the cocoon of her career apparently unscathed by her
seemingly traumatic experience. Appeals to the redemptive power
of love are as unconvincing here as those of David in *Through a Glass
Darkly*, as he walks the lonely beach with Minus, believing he has
at last found the words that work.

At the start of the 'eighties, Bergman is showing no real sign of
anything new in his art. He continues to polish his craft, which
consistently shines with technical brilliance. Yet the 'seventies saw

Still from Autumn Sonata

him repeatedly peddle the message, but less originally effectively, of *Shame* and *A Passion* about our world, as he himself puts it, 'on the slippery slope'. A weary stock of certainties prevail: sickness, confusion, guilt, despair, violence and solitude. Perhaps, however, this is an honest and fairly accurate reflection of our contemporary situation. In which case, it is all the harder on Bergman that to all intents and purposes he perfected his diagnosis in the late 'sixties, at a time of great political upheaval but when, for most of us, the prospect of continued progress, prosperity and established life style, if by no means guaranteed, seemed at least likely enough to allay our worst anxieties. The director as prophet, then, is a role that may only have served to exacerbate Bergman's own inner conflict about the nature and validity of his artistic identity. On the face of it, his unwillingness (or maybe inability) to deviate from his grim perceptions is justifiable: especially in the light of the current political, social and economic crises forcing themselves into the public's attention. Add to this the problems of mass unemployment, repressive governments and a return to the perils of a Cold War, and it may be said fairly that Bergman's prognosis is being confirmed by world events.

Bergman's equal aversion to overt political commitment and what he refers to as the 'neutralist poison' has not endeared him to those cineasts and critics, especially in Sweden, who feel that he has neglected the real concerns of the social-democratic society from which he has emerged. Even at the time of *Shame*, Bergman was accused of abstracting the realities of war by creating a false distinction between the world within and without the tortured psyches of his main characters. Bergman replied indirectly by claiming the impossibility of depicting war artistically, since 'the moral laws which come into play are quite different from those governing one's other artistic activities' (*Bergman on Bergman*, p. 235). Maria Bergom-Larson maintains that Bergman makes films from a class perspective, and that 'his limited understanding of the class structure of late capitalist society' (*Ingmar Bergman and Society*, p. 8) largely explains his artistic rut. In other words, he sees what has gone wrong but only from the idealized position of an individual artist within the hierarchical society ultimately responsible for the malaise. Hence the ambiguity of his position which nonetheless, to use his own image of a bird screeching in fear, is what drives him to successive restatements of his bleak philosophy. After all, says Larson, as head of the Royal Dramatic Theatre in Sweden during the radical activities of the late sixties, Bergman in fact showed himself simultaneously to be drawn towards the paranoid entrenchment of his protagonists whilst being repelled by their cowardice and introversion.

Yet Larson ends her sustained ideological criticism of Bergman by admiring his perspicacity in 'laying bare the anatomy of bourgeois consciousness' (p. 116). In fixing on the breakdown of our moral, social and political institutions – and in charting its devastating effect on our bodies and minds – Bergman has no peer, trapped though he may be in the frightening finality of his vision. A maker of films about private and public forms of isolation, Bergman makes of himself an isolationist, wanting to stay involved yet equally pondering the futility of action. His movement into television may well have signalled a necessary gesture towards the mass audience at a time when the majority of people need to know more of the truths about themselves, their way of life, and the ways in which their society is run and controlled.

BIBLIOGRAPHICAL NOTE

The following texts are available in English:

Filmscripts:

Four Screenplays of Ingmar Bergman (*Smiles of a Summer Night, The Seventh Seal, Wild Strawberries, The Magician*), tr. Lars Malmström and David Kushner. New York, 1960.

The Seventh Seal, tr. Malmström/Kushner. London, 1970.

Wild Strawberries, tr. Malmström/Kushner. London, 1970.

A Film Trilogy (*Through a Glass Darkly, Winter Light, The Silence*), tr. Paul Britten Austin. London, New York 1967.

Persona and Shame, tr. Keith Bradfield. London, New York 1972.

Scenes from a Marriage, tr. Alan Blair. London, 1974.

Face to Face, tr. Alan Blair. London, New York 1976.

Four Stories by Ingmar Bergman (*The Touch, Cries and Whispers, Hour of the Wolf, The Passion*), tr. Alan Blair. London, New York 1977.

The Serpent's Egg, tr. Alan Blair. London, 1978.

Autumn Sonata, tr. Alan Blair. New York, 1979.

Selected Criticism:

Bergom-Larson, Maria, *Ingmar Bergman and Society* (Film in Sweden series). London/Cranbury, New Jersey, 1978.

Björkman, Stig, Torsten Manns, and Jonas Sima (interviewers), *Bergman on Bergman*, tr. Paul Britten Austin. London, 1973.

Cowie, Peter, *Antonioni, Bergman, Resnais*. London, 1963.

Donner, Jörn, *The Personal Vision of Ingmar Bergman*, tr. Holger Lundbergh. Bloomington, Indiana, 1964.

Gibson, Arthur, *The Silence of God*. New York, 1969.

Kaminsky, Stuart M. (ed.), *Ingmar Bergman: Essays in Criticism*. London, 1975.

Simon, John, *Ingmar Bergman Directs*. New York, 1972.

Steene, Birgitta (ed.), *Focus on The Seventh Seal*. Englewood Cliffs, New Jersey, 1972.

Steene, Birgitta, *Ingmar Bergman*. New York, 1968.

Wood, Robin, *Ingmar Bergman*. London, 1967.

Young, Vernon, *Cinema Borealis: Ingmar Bergman and the Swedish Ethos*. New York, 1971.

Index